# LECTIO
# DIVINA
## OF THE
# GOSPELS

## FOR THE
## LITURGICAL YEAR
## 2019-2020

## UNITED STATES CONFERENCE OF
## CATHOLIC BISHOPS

First Printing, June 2019

ISBN 978-1-60137-627-5

# CONTENTS

*Reading seeks for the sweetness of a blessed life,*
*meditation perceives it,*
*prayer asks for it,*
*contemplation tastes it.*

*Reading, as it were, puts food whole into the mouth,*
*meditation chews it and breaks it up,*
*prayer extracts its flavor,*
*contemplation is the sweetness itself*
*which gladdens and refreshes.*

*Reading works on the outside,*
*meditation on the pith,*
*prayer asks for what we long for,*
*contemplation gives us delight in the sweetness*
*which we have found.*

— Guigo II, *The Ladder of Monks*, III (12th c.)

# What Is *Lectio Divina* and How to Use This Book

## Reading – Meditation – Prayer – Contemplation

*Lectio divina* or "divine reading" is a process of engaging with Christ, the Word of God. Through this sacred exercise, we enter into a closer relationship with the very Word himself, who communicates the love of the Father to us through the Holy Spirit.

*Lectio divina* has four steps in which we first hear what God has said (reading). We then take it in and reflect on it (meditation). From this our hearts are lifted up (prayer). Finally, after speaking to the Lord in prayer, we rest and listen for his message to us (contemplation).

This is the process of *lectio divina*. It is a conversation with God, grounded in God's own self-revelation to us. This helps us speak to God with a focus on what he has already told us about his relationship with humanity, his plans and desires for us, his promises, his admonitions, and his guidance on how we can live, so as to find true life in abundance in Christ.

Here is a brief description of each of the four steps:

# Reading (*Lectio*)

Read the passage slowly and allow it to sink in.

If there is a passage that is particularly striking, and that you want to keep with you, consider committing it to memory, or writing it down to keep with you, so that you can re-read it throughout the day, and let it enter deeper into your spirit.

*"Faith comes from what is heard, and what is heard comes through the word of Christ."* (Romans 10:17)

*"The word of God is living and effective, sharper than any two-edged sword, penetrating even between soul and spirit, joints and marrow, and able to discern reflections and thoughts of the heart."* (Hebrews 4:12)

# Meditation (*Meditatio*)

Read the passage again, and when something strikes you, a question arises in you, stop and meditate. Think about what God may be saying through it.

> *"It is the glory of God to conceal a matter,*
> *and the glory of kings to fathom a matter."*
> (Proverbs 25:2)

> *"I will ponder your precepts and consider your paths."* (Psalm 119:15)

# Prayer (*Oratio*)

Speak to the Lord about what you have read and share what's on your mind and heart—offer and share with the Lord your thanksgiving, petition, concerns, doubts, or simply affirm, back to the Lord, the very word that he has spoken.

> *"Enter his gates with thanksgiving,*
> *his courts with praise."*
> *(Psalm 100:4)*

> *"Ask and it will be given to you; seek and you will find; knock and the door will be opened to you." (Matthew 7:7)*

# Contemplation (*Contemplatio*)

This is a quiet time, a time to rest in his presence and wait upon the Lord. It is a time where we allow the Lord to speak directly to our spirit from within us. It requires practice. But this allows us to be attentive to the Lord's voice, and by regular practice, our ability to hear God's voice will grow in daily life and daily situations, as we learn to focus our minds and hearts, our thoughts, our concerns, and our hopes toward him.

> *"My sheep hear my voice; I know them, and they follow me."*
> *(John 10:27)*

> *"Be still and know that I am God!" (Psalm 46:11)*

# Applying This Process of
# *Lectio Divina* to the Liturgical Year

This *Lectio Divina of the Gospels for the Liturgical Year* book will take the reader through the Sundays and major feasts and solemnities of the liturgical year. It can be used for individual devotion and can also easily be used to assist in small group reflections in parishes and small faith groups. It offers a structured process for engaging with the Word of God. As the reader or group becomes more comfortable engaging with Scripture, this process can be more closely tailored to suit the path of growth that best fits the reader(s).

First, the *lectio divina* session is started by praying a prayer that is taken from a Mass collect from that liturgical week. Following that prayer, the main scripture passage for reflection is read, which is taken from the gospel reading for that day. This READING can be re-read, a few times, to let it sink in. Next, a set of three questions are offered to help in MEDITATION. These questions can also facilitate talking about the passage in a group setting. The individual then offers his or her personal PRAYER, responding to the Lord. In a group setting, people can speak out their prayers one at a time—this may help deepen the prayer response and further set the group's focus on the Lord.

Next, a structured set of passages and questions are offered that return the reader back to the gospel passage. This invites the reader to contemplate what the Lord is speaking and what it means for their life. It allows the individual or the prayer group to consider specific ways the Lord may be speaking into their life at that very moment. As each person begins to hear a response from the Lord—the Lord's word spoken directly and personally to them—that person can begin let that word flow through their life, by an interior change and a will to do what the Lord is asking of them. Through this step of CONTEMPLATION, we hear God's voice speaking to us, and it propels us to conversion of heart and mind.

After the closing prayer, time is given to choosing how to live out the fruit of your prayer. You know your heart and life best—if it's clear what God is asking of you, in faith, choose some way that you can put that request or teaching from the Lord into action that week. It could be a small act of faith that the Lord is asking, or perhaps, a more serious and important step that he is asking you to take. If there is nothing specific that comes to your mind, consider the question and suggestion offered in the *Living the Word This Week* section. This portion offers guidance on what concrete actions may be taken in our daily lives.

The *Lectio Divina of the Gospels for the Liturgical Year* offers a specific pattern of prayerful reading of God's Word. As you begin on this path, may the Lord's blessing follow you, and fall upon you, throughout the movement of seasons in this new liturgical year, and may your life, in turn, be a blessing upon others.

# LECTIO
# DIVINA
## OF THE
# GOSPELS

# DECEMBER 1, 2019

*Lectio Divina* for the First Week of Advent

*We begin our prayer:*
In the name of the Father, and of the Son, and of the Holy Spirit. Amen.

Keep us alert, we pray, O Lord our God,
as we await the advent of Christ your Son,
so that, when he comes and knocks,
he may find us watchful in prayer
and exultant in his praise.
Who lives and reigns with you in the unity of the Holy Spirit,
one God, for ever and ever.

*Collect, Monday of the First Week of Advent*

# Reading (*Lectio*)

*Read the following Scripture two or three times.*

Matthew 24:37-44

Jesus said to his disciples: "As it was in the days of Noah, so it will be at the coming of the Son of Man. In those days before the flood, they were eating and drinking, marrying and giving in marriage, up to the day that Noah entered the ark. They did not know until the flood came and carried them all away. So will it be also at the coming of the Son of Man. Two men will be out in the field; one will be taken, and one will be left. Two women will be grinding at the mill; one will be taken, and one will be left. Therefore, stay awake! For you do not know on which day your Lord will come. Be sure of this: if the master of the house had known the hour of night when the thief was coming, he would have stayed awake and not let his house be broken into. So too, you also must be prepared, for at an hour you do not expect, the Son of Man will come."

# Meditation (*Meditatio*)

*After the reading, take some time to reflect in silence on one or more of the following questions:*

- What word or words in this passage caught your attention?
- What in this passage comforted you?
- What in this passage challenged you?

*If practicing* lectio divina *as a family or in a group, after the reflection time, invite the participants to share their responses.*

# Prayer (*Oratio*)

*Read the Scripture passage one more time. Bring to the Lord the praise, petition, or thanksgiving that the Word inspires in you.*

# Contemplation (*Contemplatio*)

*Read the Scripture again, followed by this reflection:*

 What conversion of mind, heart, and life is the Lord asking of me?

 *Therefore, stay awake!* What distracts me from seeking to discern and know God's will? How can I be more attentive to God's active presence in my life?

 *For you do not know on which day your Lord will come.* If I knew the Lord was coming today, what would I do? What can I do today to walk more closely with God?

*So too, you also must be prepared, for at an hour you do not expect, the Son of Man will come.* How am I preparing this Advent for Jesus' coming? What do I need to do to make my heart ready to receive the Lord?

# Closing Prayer

*After a period of silent reflection and/or discussion, all recite the Lord's Prayer and the following:*

I rejoiced because they said to me,
    "We will go up to the house of the LORD."
And now we have set foot
    within your gates, O Jerusalem.

Jerusalem, built as a city
    with compact unity.
To it the tribes go up,
    the tribes of the LORD.

According to the decree for Israel,
    to give thanks to the name of the LORD.
In it are set up judgment seats,
    seats for the house of David.

Pray for the peace of Jerusalem!
    May those who love you prosper!

May peace be within your walls,
    prosperity in your buildings.

Because of my brothers and friends
    I will say, "Peace be within you!"
Because of the house of the LORD, our God,
    I will pray for your good.

*From Psalm 122*

## Living the Word This Week

*How can I make my life a gift for others in charity?*

Fast from traditional and social media as much as possible this week to allow more time for prayer and reflection.

# December 8, 2019

Lectio Divina for the Second Week of Advent

We begin our prayer:
In the name of the Father, and of the Son, and of the Holy Spirit. Amen.

May the splendor of your glory dawn in our hearts,
we pray, almighty God,
that all shadows of the night may be scattered
and we may be shown to be children of light
by the advent of your Only Begotten Son.
Who lives and reigns with you in the unity of the Holy Spirit,
one God, for ever and ever.

*Collect, Saturday of the Second Week of Advent*

# Reading (*Lectio*)

*Read the following Scripture two or three times.*

Matthew 3:1-12

John the Baptist appeared, preaching in the desert of Judea and saying, "Repent, for the kingdom of heaven is at hand!" It was of him that the prophet Isaiah had spoken when he said:

*A voice of one crying out in the desert,*
*Prepare the way of the Lord,*
*make straight his paths.*

John wore clothing made of camel's hair and had a leather belt around his waist. His food was locusts and wild honey. At that time Jerusalem, all Judea, and the whole region around the Jordan were going out to him and were being baptized by him in the Jordan River as they acknowledged their sins.

When he saw many of the Pharisees and Sadducees coming to his baptism, he said to them, "You brood of vipers! Who warned you to flee from the coming wrath? Produce good fruit as evidence of your repentance. And do not presume to say to yourselves, 'We have Abraham as our father.' For I tell you, God can raise up children to Abraham from these stones. Even now the ax lies at the root of the trees. Therefore every tree that does not bear good fruit will be cut down and thrown into the fire. I am baptizing you with water, for repentance, but the one who is coming after me is mightier than I. I am not worthy to carry his sandals. He will baptize you with the Holy Spirit and fire. His winnowing fan is in his hand. He will clear his threshing floor and gather his wheat into his barn, but the chaff he will burn with unquenchable fire."

# Meditation (*Meditatio*)

*After the reading, take some time to reflect in silence on one or more of the following questions:*

- What word or words in this passage caught your attention?
- What in this passage comforted you?
- What in this passage challenged you?

*If practicing* lectio divina *as a family or in a group, after the reflection time, invite the participants to share their responses.*

# Prayer (*Oratio*)

*Read the Scripture passage one more time. Bring to the Lord the praise, petition, or thanksgiving that the Word inspires in you.*

# Contemplation (*Contemplatio*)

*Read the Scripture again, followed by this reflection:*

 What conversion of mind, heart, and life is the Lord asking of me?

 *"Repent, for the kingdom of heaven is at hand!"* What sinful desires am I struggling to master? How can I discipline my selfish will through prayer, fasting, or other penance?

*Prepare the way of the Lord, / make straight his paths.* What crooked paths in my life need to be straightened? How can I help to address the suffering and injustice that I see around me?

 *Produce good fruit as evidence of your repentance.* What near occasions of sin do I need to avoid? How can I make amends to those I have hurt through sin and selfishness?

# Closing Prayer

*After a period of silent reflection and/or discussion, all recite the Lord's Prayer and the following:*

> I will hear what God proclaims;
>   the LORD—for he proclaims peace to his people.
> Near indeed is his salvation to those who fear him,
>   glory dwelling in our land.
>
> Kindness and truth shall meet;
>   justice and peace shall kiss.

Truth shall spring out of the earth,
    and justice shall look down from heaven.

The Lord himself will give his benefits;
    our land shall yield its increase.
Justice shall walk before him,
    and prepare the way of his steps.

*From Psalm 72*

# Living the Word This Week

*How can I make my life a gift for others in charity?*

Make plans to receive the Sacrament of Penance this Advent.

# December 9, 2019

*Lectio Divina* for the Solemnity of the
Immaculate Conception

*We begin our prayer:*
In the name of the Father, and of the Son, and of the Holy
Spirit. Amen.

O God, who by the Immaculate Conception of the Blessed
    Virgin
prepared a worthy dwelling for your Son,
grant, we pray,
that, as you preserved her from every stain
by virtue of the Death of your Son, which you foresaw,
so, through her intercession,
we, too, may be cleansed and admitted to your presence.
Through our Lord Jesus Christ, your Son,
who lives and reigns with you in the unity of the Holy Spirit,
one God, for ever and ever.

*Collect, Solemnity of the Immaculate Conception*

# Reading (*Lectio*)

*Read the following Scripture two or three times.*

Luke 1:26-38

The angel Gabriel was sent from God to a town of
Galilee called Nazareth, to a virgin betrothed to
a man named Joseph, of the house of David, and the

virgin's name was Mary. And coming to her, he said, "Hail, full of grace! The Lord is with you." But she was greatly troubled at what was said and pondered what sort of greeting this might be. Then the angel said to her, "Do not be afraid, Mary, for you have found favor with God. Behold, you will conceive in your womb and bear a son, and you shall name him Jesus. He will be great and will be called Son of the Most High, and the Lord God will give him the throne of David his father, and he will rule over the house of Jacob forever, and of his Kingdom there will be no end." But Mary said to the angel, "How can this be, since I have no relations with a man?" And the angel said to her in reply, "The Holy Spirit will come upon you, and the power of the Most High will overshadow you. Therefore the child to be born will be called holy, the Son of God. And behold, Elizabeth, your relative, has also conceived a son in her old age, and this is the sixth month for her who was called barren; for nothing will be impossible for God." Mary said, "Behold, I am the handmaid of the Lord. May it be done to me according to your word." Then the angel departed from her.

## Meditation (*Meditatio*)

*After the reading, take some time to reflect in silence on one or more of the following questions:*

- What word or words in this passage caught your attention?
- What in this passage comforted you?
- What in this passage challenged you?

*If practicing* lectio divina *as a family or in a group, after the reflection time, invite the participants to share their responses.*

# Prayer (*Oratio*)

*Read the Scripture passage one more time. Bring to the Lord the praise, petition, or thanksgiving that the Word inspires in you.*

# Contemplation (*Contemplatio*)

*Read the Scripture again, followed by this reflection:*

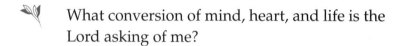

What conversion of mind, heart, and life is the Lord asking of me?

*For you have found favor with God.* How has God blessed me with his favor this week? Am I attentive to the blessings that God has poured out on me?

*How can this be?* When has God surprised or amazed me? Upon whom can I rely for good answers to my questions?

 *Therefore the child to be born will be called holy, the Son of God.* Do I give God due honor for his holiness? Am I reverent?

# Closing Prayer

*After a period of silent reflection and/or discussion, all recite the Lord's Prayer and the following:*

Sing to the LORD a new song,
   for he has done wondrous deeds;
His right hand has won victory for him,
   his holy arm.

The LORD has made his salvation known:
   in the sight of the nations he has revealed his justice.
He has remembered his kindness and his faithfulness
   toward the house of Israel.

All the ends of the earth have seen
    the salvation by our God.
Sing joyfully to the Lord, all you lands;
    break into song; sing praise.

*From Psalm 98*

# Living the Word This Week

*How can I make my life a gift for others in charity?*

Spend some time this week in prayer before the
Blessed Sacrament.

# DECEMBER 15, 2019

*Lectio Divina* for the Third Week of Advent

*We begin our prayer:*
In the name of the Father, and of the Son, and of the Holy
Spirit. Amen.

O God, who through your Only Begotten Son
have made us a new creation,
look kindly, we pray,
on the handiwork of your mercy,
and at your Son's coming
cleanse us from every stain of the old way of life.
Through our Lord Jesus Christ, your Son,
who lives and reigns with you in the unity of the Holy Spirit,
one God, for ever and ever.

*Collect, Tuesday of the Third Week of Advent*

# Reading (*Lectio*)

*Read the following Scripture two or three times.*

Matthew 11:2-11

When John the Baptist heard in prison of the
works of the Christ, he sent his disciples to
Jesus with this question, "Are you the one who is to
come, or should we look for another?" Jesus said to
them in reply, "Go and tell John what you hear and
see: the blind regain their sight, the lame walk, lepers

16

are cleansed, the deaf hear, the dead are raised, and the poor have the good news proclaimed to them. And blessed is the one who takes no offense at me."

As they were going off, Jesus began to speak to the crowds about John, "What did you go out to the desert to see? A reed swayed by the wind? Then what did you go out to see? Someone dressed in fine clothing? Those who wear fine clothing are in royal palaces. Then why did you go out? To see a prophet? Yes, I tell you, and more than a prophet. This is the one about whom it is written:

*Behold, I am sending my messenger ahead of you;*
*    he will prepare your way before you.*

Amen, I say to you, among those born of women there has been none greater than John the Baptist; yet the least in the kingdom of heaven is greater than he."

# Meditation (*Meditatio*)

*After the reading, take some time to reflect in silence on one or more of the following questions:*

- What word or words in this passage caught your attention?
- What in this passage comforted you?
- What in this passage challenged you?

*If practicing* lectio divina *as a family or in a group, after the reflection time, invite the participants to share their responses.*

# Prayer (*Oratio*)

*Read the Scripture passage one more time. Bring to the Lord the praise, petition, or thanksgiving that the Word inspires in you.*

# Contemplation (*Contemplatio*)

*Read the Scripture again, followed by this reflection:*

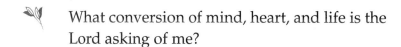 What conversion of mind, heart, and life is the Lord asking of me?

 *Are you the one who is to come, or should we look for another?* Where do I go to feel God's presence? When am I most aware of God acting in my life?

*The poor have the good news proclaimed to them.* How can I accompany the poor and those at the margins? How do I proclaim the good news in my words and actions?

 *Yet the least in the kingdom of heaven is greater than he.* What does it mean to be great in the sight of God? How do the world's values distort my understanding of what it means to be great?

# Closing Prayer

*After a period of silent reflection and/or discussion, all recite the Lord's Prayer and the following:*

The LORD God keeps faith forever,
    secures justice for the oppressed,
    gives food to the hungry.
The LORD sets captives free.

The LORD gives sight to the blind;
    the LORD raises up those who were bowed down.

The Lord loves the just;
    the Lord protects strangers.

The fatherless and the widow he sustains,
    but the way of the wicked he thwarts.
The Lord shall reign forever;
    your God, O Zion, through all generations.

*From Psalm 146*

# Living the Word This Week

*How can I make my life a gift for others in charity?*

In this season of giving, donate your time, treasure, or talent to those in need.

# December 22, 2019

*Lectio Divina* for the Fourth Week of Advent

*We begin our prayer:*

In the name of the Father, and of the Son, and of the Holy Spirit. Amen.

Come quickly, we pray, Lord Jesus,
and do not delay,
that those who trust in your compassion
may find solace and relief in your coming.
Who live and reign with God the Father
in the unity of the Holy Spirit,
one God, for ever and ever.

*Collect, December 24, Mass in the Morning*

# Reading (*Lectio*)

*Read the following Scripture two or three times.*

Matthew 1:18-24

This is how the birth of Jesus Christ came about. When his mother Mary was betrothed to Joseph, but before they lived together, she was found with child through the Holy Spirit. Joseph her husband, since he was a righteous man, yet unwilling to expose her to shame, decided to divorce her quietly. Such was his intention when, behold, the angel of the Lord appeared to him in a dream and said, "Joseph, son of David, do not be afraid to take Mary your wife into your home. For it is through the Holy Spirit that this child has been conceived in her. She will bear a son and you are to name him Jesus, because he will save his people from their sins." All this took place to fulfill what the Lord had said through the prophet:

*Behold, the virgin shall conceive and bear a son,*
*and they shall name him Emmanuel,*

which means "God is with us." When Joseph awoke, he did as the angel of the Lord had commanded him and took his wife into his home.

# Meditation (*Meditatio*)

*After the reading, take some time to reflect in silence on one or more of the following questions:*

- What word or words in this passage caught your attention?
- What in this passage comforted you?
- What in this passage challenged you?

*If practicing* lectio divina *as a family or in a group, after the reflection time, invite the participants to share their responses.*

# Prayer (*Oratio*)

*Read the Scripture passage one more time. Bring to the Lord the praise, petition, or thanksgiving that the Word inspires in you.*

# Contemplation (*Contemplatio*)

*Read the Scripture again, followed by this reflection:*

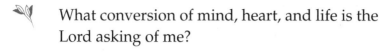 What conversion of mind, heart, and life is the Lord asking of me?

*Joseph . . . was a righteous man.* How do my actions testify to my faith? How can I be more active in pursuing justice and righteousness?

*Do not be afraid.* What fears keep me from following God's will for me? How can I grow in trust of God's loving providence?

*He did as the angel of the Lord had commanded him.*
How do I discern what God is calling me to
do? How can I have the courage and discipline
needed to follow God's commands?

# Closing Prayer

*After a period of silent reflection and/or discussion, all recite the
Lord's Prayer and the following:*

The LORD's are the earth and its fullness;
   the world and those who dwell in it.
For he founded it upon the seas
   and established it upon the rivers.

Who can ascend the mountain of the LORD?
   or who may stand in his holy place?
One whose hands are sinless, whose heart is clean,
   who desires not what is vain.

He shall receive a blessing from the LORD,
   a reward from God his savior.
Such is the race that seeks for him,
   that seeks the face of the God of Jacob.

*From Psalm 24*

# Living the Word This Week

*How can I make my life a gift for others in charity?*

Support families facing difficult pregnancies with prayer and support for local pro-life agencies.

# December 25, 2019

*Lectio Divina* for the Solemnity of Christmas

*We begin our prayer:*
In the name of the Father, and of the Son, and of the Holy Spirit. Amen.

Grant, we pray, almighty God,
that, as we are bathed in the new radiance of your incarnate Word,
the light of faith, which illumines our minds,
may also shine through in our deeds.
Through our Lord Jesus Christ, your Son,
who lives and reigns with you in the unity of the Holy Spirit,
one God, for ever and ever.

*Collect, Christmas, Mass at Dawn*

# Reading (*Lectio*)

*Read the following Scripture two or three times.*

Luke 2:1-14

In those days a decree went out from Caesar Augustus that the whole world should be enrolled. This was the first enrollment, when Quirinius was governor of Syria. So all went to be enrolled, each to his own town. And Joseph too went up from Galilee from the town of Nazareth to Judea, to the city of David that is called Bethlehem, because he was of the house and family of David, to be enrolled with Mary, his betrothed, who was with child. While they were there, the time came for her to have her child, and she gave birth to her firstborn son. She wrapped him in swaddling clothes and laid him in a manger, because there was no room for them in the inn.

Now there were shepherds in that region living in the fields and keeping the night watch over their flock. The angel of the Lord appeared to them and the glory of the Lord shone around them, and they were struck with great fear. The angel said to them, "Do not be afraid; for behold, I proclaim to you good news of great joy that will be for all the people. For today in the city of David a savior has been born for you who is Christ and Lord. And this will be a sign for you: you will find an infant wrapped in swaddling clothes and lying in a manger."

And suddenly there was a multitude of the heavenly host with the angel, praising God and saying:

"Glory to God in the highest
    and on earth peace to those on whom his favor rests."

# Meditation (*Meditatio*)

*After the reading, take some time to reflect in silence on one or more of the following questions:*

- What word or words in this passage caught your attention?
- What in this passage comforted you?
- What in this passage challenged you?

*If practicing* lectio divina *as a family or in a group, after the reflection time, invite the participants to share their responses.*

# Prayer (*Oratio*)

*Read the Scripture passage one more time. Bring to the Lord the praise, petition, or thanksgiving that the Word inspires in you.*

# Contemplation (*Contemplatio*)

*Read the Scripture again, followed by this reflection:*

 What conversion of mind, heart, and life is the Lord asking of me?

 *So all went to be enrolled, each to his own town.* How engaged am I with my parish faith community? How can I be more welcoming of those who seek a place to belong?

*Now there were shepherds in that region living in the fields and keeping the night watch over their flock.* How can I follow the shepherds' example of simplicity and vigilance? Over whom should I keep watch in prayer?

 *For behold, I proclaim to you good news of great joy that will be for all the people.* How can I express the joy that comes from my faith? How does my life proclaim good news to those around me?

# Closing Prayer

*After a period of silent reflection and/or discussion, all recite the Lord's Prayer and the following:*

Sing to the LORD a new song;
     sing to the LORD, all you lands.
Sing to the LORD; bless his name.

Announce his salvation, day after day.
     Tell his glory among the nations;
     among all peoples, his wondrous deeds.

Let the heavens be glad and the earth rejoice;
     let the sea and what fills it resound;
     let the plains be joyful and all that is in them!
Then shall all the trees of the forest exult.

They shall exult before the LORD, for he comes;
     for he comes to rule the earth.
He shall rule the world with justice
     and the peoples with his constancy.

*From Psalm 96*

# Living the Word This Week

*How can I make my life a gift for others in charity?*

Reach out to someone who is lonely or depressed in this holiday season.

# December 29, 2019

*Lectio Divina* for the Feast of the Holy Family of Jesus, Mary, and Joseph

*We begin our prayer:*
In the name of the Father, and of the Son, and of the Holy Spirit. Amen.

O God, who were pleased to give us
the shining example of the Holy Family,
graciously grant that we may imitate them
in practicing the virtues of family life and in the bonds
   of charity,
and so, in the joy of your house,
delight one day in eternal rewards.
Through our Lord Jesus Christ, your Son,
who lives and reigns with you in the unity of the Holy Spirit,
one God, for ever and ever.

*Collect, Feast of the Holy Family*

# Reading (*Lectio*)

*Read the following Scripture two or three times.*

Matthew 2:13-15, 19-23

When the magi had departed, behold, the angel of the Lord appeared to Joseph in a dream and said, "Rise, take the child and his mother, flee to Egypt, and stay there until I tell you.

Herod is going to search for the child to destroy him."
Joseph rose and took the child and his mother by night
and departed for Egypt. He stayed there until the
death of Herod, that what the Lord had said through
the prophet might be fulfilled,

*Out of Egypt I called my son.*

When Herod had died, behold, the angel of the Lord
appeared in a dream to Joseph in Egypt and said,
"Rise, take the child and his mother and go to the
land of Israel, for those who sought the child's life are
dead." He rose, took the child and his mother, and
went to the land of Israel. But when he heard that
Archelaus was ruling over Judea in place of his father
Herod, he was afraid to go back there. And because
he had been warned in a dream, he departed for the
region of Galilee. He went and dwelt in a town called
Nazareth, so that what had been spoken through the
prophets might be fulfilled,

*He shall be called a Nazorean.*


# Meditation (*Meditatio*)

*After the reading, take some time to reflect in silence on one or more
of the following questions:*

- What word or words in this passage caught
  your attention?
- What in this passage comforted you?
- What in this passage challenged you?

*If practicing* lectio divina *as a family or in a group, after the
reflection time, invite the participants to share their responses.*

# Prayer (*Oratio*)

*Read the Scripture passage one more time. Bring to the Lord the praise, petition, or thanksgiving that the Word inspires in you.*

# Contemplation (*Contemplatio*)

*Read the Scripture again, followed by this reflection:*

 What conversion of mind, heart, and life is the Lord asking of me?

 *Behold, the angel of the Lord appeared to Joseph in a dream.* How and where do I hear the voice of God? How can I be more attentive to the voice of God?

*Rise, take the child and his mother, flee to Egypt, and stay there until I tell you.* Where is God calling me to go? What will I need for this journey?

 *He was afraid to go back there.* What parts of my past do I need to bring to God for healing? What bad habits do I need to leave behind?

# Closing Prayer

*After a period of silent reflection and/or discussion, all recite the Lord's Prayer and the following:*

> Blessed is everyone who fears the LORD,
>     who walks in his ways!
> For you shall eat the fruit of your handiwork;
>     blessed shall you be, and favored.
>
> Your wife shall be like a fruitful vine
>     in the recesses of your home;
> your children like olive plant
>     around your table.

Behold, thus is the man blessed
　　who fears the Lord.
The Lord bless you from Zion:
　　may you see the prosperity of Jerusalem
　　all the days of your life.

*From Psalm 128*

# Living the Word This Week

*How can I make my life a gift for others in charity?*

Read and reflect on paragraph numbers 90-119
in *Amoris Laetitia: http://w2.vatican.va/content/
dam/francesco/pdf/apost_exhortations/documents/
papa-francesco_esortazione-ap_20160319_amoris-laetitia_en.pdf.*

# January 1, 2020

*Lectio Divina* for the Solemnity of Mary, Mother of God

*We begin our prayer:*
In the name of the Father, and of the Son, and of the Holy
Spirit. Amen.

Almighty ever-living God,
splendor of faithful souls,
graciously be pleased to fill the world with your glory,
and show yourself to all peoples by the radiance of your light.
Through our Lord Jesus Christ, your Son,
who lives and reigns with you in the unity of the Holy Spirit,
one God, for ever and ever.

*Collect, Second Sunday after the Nativity*

# Reading (*Lectio*)

*Read the following Scripture two or three times.*

Luke 2:16-21

The shepherds went in haste to Bethlehem and
found Mary and Joseph, and the infant lying in
the manger. When they saw this, they made known
the message that had been told them about this child.
All who heard it were amazed by what had been
told them by the shepherds. And Mary kept all these
things, reflecting on them in her heart. Then the
shepherds returned, glorifying and praising God for

all they had heard and seen, just as it had been told to them.

When eight days were completed for his circumcision, he was named Jesus, the name given him by the angel before he was conceived in the womb.

# Meditation (*Meditatio*)

*After the reading, take some time to reflect in silence on one or more of the following questions:*

- What word or words in this passage caught your attention?
- What in this passage comforted you?
- What in this passage challenged you?

*If practicing* lectio divina *as a family or in a group, after the reflection time, invite the participants to share their responses.*

# Prayer (*Oratio*)

*Read the Scripture passage one more time. Bring to the Lord the praise, petition, or thanksgiving that the Word inspires in you.*

# Contemplation (*Contemplatio*)

*Read the Scripture again, followed by this reflection:*

 What conversion of mind, heart, and life is the Lord asking of me?

*The shepherds went in haste to Bethlehem and found Mary and Joseph, and the infant lying in the manger.* How can I make spending time in God's presence a priority? Do I hasten to follow God's will or look for reasons to delay?

*Then the shepherds returned, glorifying and praising God for all they had heard and seen.* For what do I give God thanks and praise? How have I seen and heard God this week?

He was named Jesus, the name given him by the angel before he was conceived in the womb. How did I first learn about God? Who nurtured my faith in its earliest days?

# Closing Prayer

*After a period of silent reflection and/or discussion, all recite the Lord's Prayer and the following:*

May God have pity on us and bless us;
    may he let his face shine upon us.
So may your way be known upon earth;
    among all nations, your salvation.

May the nations be glad and exult
    because you rule the peoples in equity;
    the nations on the earth you guide.

May the peoples praise you, O God;
    may all the peoples praise you!
May God bless us,
    and may all the ends of the earth fear him!

*From Psalm 67*

# Living the Word This Week

*How can I make my life a gift for others in charity?*

Make a resolution to pray every day.

# January 5, 2020

*Lectio Divina* for the Solemnity of the Epiphany

*We begin our prayer:*

In the name of the Father, and of the Son, and of the Holy Spirit. Amen.

O God, who through your Son raised up your eternal light for
    all nations,
grant that your people may come to acknowledge
the full splendor of their Redeemer,
that, bathed ever more in his radiance,
they may reach everlasting glory.
Through our Lord Jesus Christ, your Son,
who lives and reigns with you in the unity of the Holy Spirit,
one God, for ever and ever.

*Collect, Thursday after the Epiphany*

# Reading (*Lectio*)

*Read the following Scripture two or three times.*

Matthew 2:1-12

When Jesus was born in Bethlehem of Judea, in the days of King Herod, behold, magi from the east arrived in Jerusalem, saying, "Where is the newborn king of the Jews? We saw his star at its rising and have come to do him homage." When King Herod heard this, he was greatly troubled, and all Jerusalem with him. Assembling all the chief priests and the scribes of the people, he inquired of them where the Christ was to be born. They said to him, "In Bethlehem of Judea, for thus it has been written through the prophet:

*And you, Bethlehem, land of Judah,*
*    are by no means least among the rulers of Judah;*
*since from you shall come a ruler,*
*    who is to shepherd my people Israel."*

Then Herod called the magi secretly and ascertained from them the time of the star's appearance. He sent them to Bethlehem and said, "Go and search diligently for the child. When you have found him, bring me word, that I too may go and do him homage." After their audience with the king they set out. And behold, the star that they had seen at its rising preceded them, until it came and stopped over the place where the child was. They were overjoyed at seeing the star, and on entering the house they saw the child with Mary his mother. They prostrated themselves and did him homage. Then they opened their treasures and offered him gifts of gold, frankincense, and myrrh. And having been warned in a dream not to return to Herod, they departed for their country by another way.

# Meditation (*Meditatio*)

*After the reading, take some time to reflect in silence on one or more of the following questions:*

- What word or words in this passage caught your attention?
- What in this passage comforted you?
- What in this passage challenged you?

*If practicing* lectio divina *as a family or in a group, after the reflection time, invite the participants to share their responses.*

# Prayer (*Oratio*)

*Read the Scripture passage one more time. Bring to the Lord the praise, petition, or thanksgiving that the Word inspires in you.*

# Contemplation (*Contemplatio*)

*Read the Scripture again, followed by this reflection:*

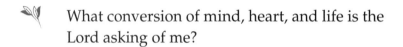

What conversion of mind, heart, and life is the Lord asking of me?

*Where is the newborn king of the Jews?* How can I help others encounter Christ? How can I accompany them on their journey to him?

*Then they opened their treasures and offered him gifts of gold, frankincense, and myrrh.* What do I treasure? How do I share my gifts with those in need?

 *And having been warned in a dream not to return to Herod, they departed for their country by another way.* Whom can I rely on to warn me away from danger and sin? Who gives me an example of following God's way?

# Closing Prayer

*After a period of silent reflection and/or discussion, all recite the Lord's Prayer and the following:*

> O God, with your judgment endow the king,
>     and with your justice, the king's son;
> He shall govern your people with justice
>     and your afflicted ones with judgment.

Justice shall flower in his days,
  and profound peace, till the moon be no more.
May he rule from sea to sea,
  and from the River to the ends of the earth.

The kings of Tarshish and the Isles shall offer gifts;
  the kings of Arabia and Seba shall bring tribute.
All kings shall pay him homage,
  all nations shall serve him.

For he shall rescue the poor when he cries out,
  and the afflicted when he has no one to help him.
He shall have pity for the lowly and the poor;
  the lives of the poor he shall save.

*From Psalm 72*

# Living the Word This Week

*How can I make my life a gift for others in charity?*

During this National Migration Week, learn how you can help immigrants and refugees: *www.usccb.org/about/migration-and-refugee-services/national-migration-week/index.cfm.*

# January 12, 2020

*Lectio Divina* for Feast of the Baptism of the Lord

*We begin our prayer:*
In the name of the Father, and of the Son, and of the Holy
Spirit. Amen.

Almighty ever-living God,
who, when Christ had been baptized in the River Jordan
and as the Holy Spirit descended upon him,
solemnly declared him your beloved Son,
grant that your children by adoption,
reborn of water and the Holy Spirit,
may always be well pleasing to you.
Through our Lord Jesus Christ, your Son,
who lives and reigns with you in the unity of the Holy Spirit,
one God, for ever and ever.

*Collect, Feast of the Baptism of the Lord*

# Reading (*Lectio*)

*Read the following Scripture two or three times.*

Matthew 3:13-17

Jesus came from Galilee to John at the Jordan to be
baptized by him. John tried to prevent him, saying,
"I need to be baptized by you, and yet you are coming
to me?" Jesus said to him in reply, "Allow it now, for
thus it is fitting for us to fulfill all righteousness." Then

he allowed him. After Jesus was baptized, he came up from the water and behold, the heavens were opened for him, and he saw the Spirit of God descending like a dove and coming upon him. And a voice came from the heavens, saying, "This is my beloved Son, with whom I am well pleased."

# Meditation (*Meditatio*)

*After the reading, take some time to reflect in silence on one or more of the following questions:*

- What word or words in this passage caught your attention?
- What in this passage comforted you?
- What in this passage challenged you?

*If practicing* lectio divina *as a family or in a group, after the reflection time, invite the participants to share their responses.*

# Prayer (*Oratio*)

*Read the Scripture passage one more time. Bring to the Lord the praise, petition, or thanksgiving that the Word inspires in you.*

# Contemplation (*Contemplatio*)

*Read the Scripture again, followed by this reflection:*

 What conversion of mind, heart, and life is the Lord asking of me?

*John tried to prevent him.* What obstacles keep me from following Jesus wholeheartedly? How do my actions prevent others from coming to Christ?

*Allow it now, for thus it is fitting for us to fulfill all righteousness.* What commandments of God do I struggle to follow? How can I help to create a culture of justice and righteousness?

*He came up from the water and behold, the heavens were opened for him.* When have I experienced God's majesty and power? What do I hope that heaven will be like?

# Closing Prayer

*After a period of silent reflection and/or discussion, all recite the Lord's Prayer and the following:*

Give to the LORD, you sons of God,
　　give to the LORD glory and praise,
Give to the LORD the glory due his name;
　　adore the LORD in holy attire.

The voice of the LORD is over the waters,
　　the LORD, over vast waters.
The voice of the LORD is mighty;
　　the voice of the LORD is majestic.

The God of glory thunders,
　　and in his temple all say, "Glory!"
The LORD is enthroned above the flood;
　　the LORD is enthroned as king forever.

*From Psalm 29*


# Living the Word This Week

*How can I make my life a gift for others in charity?*

Continue to learn more about your faith by attending a class in your parish or diocese or by reading good Catholic books.

# JANUARY 19, 2020

*Lectio Divina* for the Second Week in Ordinary Time

*We begin our prayer:*

In the name of the Father, and of the Son, and of the Holy Spirit. Amen.

Almighty ever-living God,
who govern all things,
both in heaven and on earth,
mercifully hear the pleading of your people
and bestow your peace on our times.
Through our Lord Jesus Christ, your Son,
who lives and reigns with you in the unity of the Holy Spirit,
one God, for ever and ever.

*Collect, Second Sunday in Ordinary Time*

# Reading (*Lectio*)

*Read the following Scripture two or three times.*

John 1:29-34

John the Baptist saw Jesus coming toward him and said, "Behold, the Lamb of God, who takes away the sin of the world. He is the one of whom I said, 'A man is coming after me who ranks ahead of me because he existed before me.' I did not know him, but the reason why I came baptizing with water was that he might be made known to Israel." John testified further, saying, "I saw the Spirit come down like a dove from heaven and remain upon him. I did not know him, but the one who sent me to baptize with water told me, 'On whomever you see the Spirit come down and remain, he is the one who will baptize with the Holy Spirit.' Now I have seen and testified that he is the Son of God."

# Meditation (*Meditatio*)

*After the reading, take some time to reflect in silence on one or more of the following questions:*

- What word or words in this passage caught your attention?
- What in this passage comforted you?
- What in this passage challenged you?

*If practicing* lectio divina *as a family or in a group, after the reflection time, invite the participants to share their responses.*

# Prayer (*Oratio*)

*Read the Scripture passage one more time. Bring to the Lord the praise, petition, or thanksgiving that the Word inspires in you.*

# Contemplation (*Contemplatio*)

*Read the Scripture again, followed by this reflection:*

 What conversion of mind, heart, and life is the Lord asking of me?

*Behold, the Lamb of God, who takes away the sin of the world.* What sins do I need to ask God to forgive in his mercy? How am I open to God's grace working in me to take away sin?

*A man is coming after me who ranks ahead of me because he existed before me.* What prejudices or biases do I bring to my interactions with others? How can I more intentionally see Christ in those I meet?

*Now I have seen and testified that he is the Son of God.* What people, places, and events strengthen my faith? How can I share my faith in Christ with those I meet?

# Closing Prayer

*After a period of silent reflection and/or discussion, all recite the Lord's Prayer and the following:*

I have waited, waited for the LORD,
    and he stooped toward me and heard my cry.
And he put a new song into my mouth,
    a hymn to our God.

Sacrifice or offering you wished not,
    but ears open to obedience you gave me.
Holocausts or sin-offerings you sought not;
    then said I, "Behold I come."

"In the written scroll it is prescribed for me,
to do your will, O my God, is my delight,
    and your law is within my heart!"

I announced your justice in the vast assembly;
    I did not restrain my lips, as you, O LORD, know.

*From Psalm 40*

# Living the Word This Week

*How can I make my life a gift for others in charity?*

Share your faith with someone this week: in conversation, in writing, or in an invitation to Mass.

# January 26, 2020

Lectio Divina for the Third Week in Ordinary Time

We begin our prayer:
In the name of the Father, and of the Son, and of the Holy
Spirit. Amen.

Almighty ever-living God,
direct our actions according to your good pleasure,
that in the name of your beloved Son
we may abound in good works.
Through our Lord Jesus Christ, your Son,
who lives and reigns with you in the unity of the Holy Spirit,
one God, for ever and ever.

*Collect, Third Sunday in Ordinary Time*

# Reading (*Lectio*)

*Read the following Scripture two or three times.*

Matthew 4:12-23

When Jesus heard that John had been arrested,
he withdrew to Galilee. He left Nazareth and
went to live in Capernaum by the sea, in the region
of Zebulun and Naphtali, that what had been said
through Isaiah the prophet might be fulfilled:

*Land of Zebulun and land of Naphtali,
  the way to the sea, beyond the Jordan,*

*Galilee of the Gentiles,*
*the people who sit in darkness have seen a great light,*
*on those dwelling in a land overshadowed by death*
    *light has arisen.*

From that time on, Jesus began to preach and say, "Repent, for the kingdom of heaven is at hand."

As he was walking by the Sea of Galilee, he saw two brothers, Simon who is called Peter, and his brother Andrew, casting a net into the sea; they were fishermen. He said to them, "Come after me, and I will make you fishers of men." At once they left their nets and followed him. He walked along from there and saw two other brothers, James, the son of Zebedee, and his brother John. They were in a boat, with their father Zebedee, mending their nets. He called them, and immediately they left their boat and their father and followed him. He went around all of Galilee, teaching in their synagogues, proclaiming the gospel of the kingdom, and curing every disease and illness among the people.

# Meditation (*Meditatio*)

*After the reading, take some time to reflect in silence on one or more of the following questions:*

- What word or words in this passage caught your attention?
- What in this passage comforted you?
- What in this passage challenged you?

*If practicing* lectio divina *as a family or in a group, after the reflection time, invite the participants to share their responses.*

# Prayer (*Oratio*)

*Read the Scripture passage one more time. Bring to the Lord the praise, petition, or thanksgiving that the Word inspires in you.*

# Contemplation (*Contemplatio*)

*Read the Scripture again, followed by this reflection:*

 What conversion of mind, heart, and life is the Lord asking of me?

 *When Jesus heard that John had been arrested, he withdrew to Galilee.* What distracts me from prayer? Where can I go to pray without distraction?

*He called them, and immediately they left their boat and their father and followed him.* What do I need to leave behind to follow Jesus? To what is God calling me?

*He went around all of Galilee, teaching in their synagogues, proclaiming the gospel of the kingdom, and curing every disease and illness among the people.* How do I put my faith in action in my daily life? How can I serve those around me?

# Closing Prayer

*After a period of silent reflection and/or discussion, all recite the Lord's Prayer and the following:*

The LORD is my light and my salvation;
    whom should I fear?
The LORD is my life's refuge;
    of whom should I be afraid?

One thing I ask of the LORD;
   this I seek:
To dwell in the house of the LORD
   all the days of my life,
That I may gaze on the loveliness of the LORD
   and contemplate his temple.

I believe that I shall see the bounty of the LORD
   in the land of the living.
Wait for the LORD with courage;
   be stouthearted, and wait for the LORD.

*From Psalm 27*

# Living the Word This Week

*How can I make my life a gift for others in charity?*

Learn about the various ministry and volunteer opportunities offered in your parish and choose how to offer your gifts in loving service.

# February 2, 2020

*Lectio Divina* for the Presentation of the Lord

*We begin our prayer:*

In the name of the Father, and of the Son, and of the Holy Spirit. Amen.

Almighty ever-living God,
we humbly implore your majesty
that, just as your Only Begotten Son
was presented on this day in the Temple
in the substance of our flesh,
so, by your grace,
we may be presented to you with minds made pure.
Through our Lord Jesus Christ, your Son,
who lives and reigns with you in the unity of the Holy Spirit,
one God, for ever and ever.

*Collect, Feast of the Presentation of the Lord*

# Reading (*Lectio*)

*Read the following Scripture two or three times.*

Luke 2:22-40

When the days were completed for their purification according to the law of Moses, Mary and Joseph took Jesus up to Jerusalem to present him to the Lord, just as it is written in the law of the Lord,

*Every male that opens the womb shall be consecrated to the Lord*, and to offer the sacrifice of *a pair of turtledoves or two young pigeons*, in accordance with the dictate in the law of the Lord.

Now there was a man in Jerusalem whose name was Simeon. This man was righteous and devout, awaiting the consolation of Israel, and the Holy Spirit was upon him. It had been revealed to him by the Holy Spirit that he should not see death before he had seen the Christ of the Lord. He came in the Spirit into the temple; and when the parents brought in the child Jesus to perform the custom of the law in regard to him, he took him into his arms and blessed God, saying:

"Now, Master, you may let your servant go
     in peace, according to your word,
for my eyes have seen your salvation,
     which you prepared in the sight of all the peoples:
a light for revelation to the Gentiles,
     and glory for your people Israel."

The child's father and mother were amazed at what was said about him; and Simeon blessed them and said to Mary his mother, "Behold, this child is destined for the fall and rise of many in Israel, and to be a sign that will be contradicted—and you yourself a sword will pierce—so that the thoughts of many hearts may be revealed." There was also a prophetess, Anna, the daughter of Phanuel, of the tribe of Asher. She was advanced in years, having lived seven years with her husband after her marriage, and then as a widow until she was eighty-four. She never left the temple, but worshiped night and day with fasting and prayer. And

coming forward at that very time, she gave thanks
to God and spoke about the child to all who were
awaiting the redemption of Jerusalem.

When they had fulfilled all the prescriptions of the law
of the Lord, they returned to Galilee, to their own town
of Nazareth. The child grew and became strong, filled
with wisdom; and the favor of God was upon him.

# Meditation (*Meditatio*)

*After the reading, take some time to reflect in silence on one or more
of the following questions:*

- What word or words in this passage caught
  your attention?
- What in this passage comforted you?
- What in this passage challenged you?

*If practicing* lectio divina *as a family or in a group, after the
reflection time, invite the participants to share their responses.*

# Prayer (*Oratio*)

*Read the Scripture passage one more time. Bring to the Lord the
praise, petition, or thanksgiving that the Word inspires in you.*

# Contemplation (*Contemplatio*)

*Read the Scripture again, followed by this reflection:*

 What conversion of mind, heart, and life is the Lord asking of me?

 *This man was righteous and devout, awaiting the consolation of Israel, and the Holy Spirit was upon him.* What are you waiting for God to do? What are the sources of your hope?

*Behold, this child is destined for the fall and rise of many in Israel, and to be a sign that will be contradicted—and you yourself a sword will pierce—so that the thoughts of many hearts may be revealed.* In what ways has your faith been in conflict with the values of the world around you? What graces do you need to stand strong in faith?

 *And coming forward at that very time, she gave thanks to God and spoke about the child to all who were awaiting the redemption of Jerusalem.* What has God done for you that you would like to share with others? When was the last time you talked to someone about your faith?

# Closing Prayer

*After a period of silent reflection and/or discussion, all recite the Lord's Prayer and the following:*

Lift up, O gates, your lintels;
    reach up, you ancient portals,
    that the king of glory may come in!

Who is this king of glory?
    The LORD, strong and mighty,
    the LORD, mighty in battle.

Lift up, O gates, your lintels;
    reach up, you ancient portals,
    that the king of glory may come in!

Who is this king of glory?
    The LORD of hosts; he is the king of glory.

*From Psalm 24*

# Living the Word This Week

*How can I make my life a gift for others in charity?*

Find out how your parish supports young families and/or families in crisis and contribute to this effort with your time or your prayers.

# FEBRUARY 9, 2020

*Lectio Divina* for the Fifth Week in Ordinary Time

*We begin our prayer:*
In the name of the Father, and of the Son, and of the Holy
Spirit. Amen.

Keep your family safe, O Lord, with unfailing care,
that, relying solely on the hope of heavenly grace,
they may be defended always by your protection.
Through our Lord Jesus Christ, your Son,
who lives and reigns with you in the unity of the Holy Spirit,
one God, for ever and ever.

*Collect, Fifth Sunday in Ordinary Time*

# Reading (*Lectio*)

*Read the following Scripture two or three times.*

Matthew 5:13-16

Jesus said to his disciples: "You are the salt of the
earth. But if salt loses its taste, with what can it be
seasoned? It is no longer good for anything but to
be thrown out and trampled underfoot. You are the
light of the world. A city set on a mountain cannot be
hidden. Nor do they light a lamp and then put it under
a bushel basket; it is set on a lampstand, where it gives
light to all in the house. Just so, your light must shine
before others, that they may see your good deeds and
glorify your heavenly Father."

# Meditation (*Meditatio*)

*After the reading, take some time to reflect in silence on one or more of the following questions:*

- What word or words in this passage caught your attention?
- What in this passage comforted you?
- What in this passage challenged you?

*If practicing* lectio divina *as a family or in a group, after the reflection time, invite the participants to share their responses.*

# Prayer (*Oratio*)

*Read the Scripture passage one more time. Bring to the Lord the praise, petition, or thanksgiving that the Word inspires in you.*

# Contemplation (*Contemplatio*)

*Read the Scripture again, followed by this reflection:*

 What conversion of mind, heart, and life is the Lord asking of me?

 *But if salt loses its taste, with what can it be seasoned?* What people, places, and things

re-invigorate your faith? How often do you
express your joy and enthusiasm for your faith?

*You are the light of the world.* How can I bring light
and truth into my interactions with others? How
can I learn to see others through the eyes of God?

*Just so, your light must shine before others, that they
may see your good deeds and glorify your heavenly
Father.* How does the way I live reflect what
I believe? In what ways am I a good or bad
example for those who are seeking God?

# Closing Prayer

*After a period of silent reflection and/or discussion, all recite the Lord's Prayer and the following:*

Light shines through the darkness for the upright;
>    he is gracious and merciful and just.
Well for the man who is gracious and lends,
>    who conducts his affairs with justice.

He shall never be moved;
>    the just one shall be in everlasting remembrance.
An evil report he shall not fear;
>    his heart is firm, trusting in the LORD.

His heart is steadfast; he shall not fear.
>    Lavishly he gives to the poor;
His justice shall endure forever;
>    his horn shall be exalted in glory.

*From Psalm 112*

# Living the Word This Week

*How can I make my life a gift for others in charity?*

Join the issue advocacy network of your diocese or state Catholic conference.

# February 16, 2020

*Lectio Divina* for the Sixth Week in Ordinary Time

*We begin our prayer:*
In the name of the Father, and of the Son, and of the Holy
Spirit. Amen.

O God, who teach us that you abide
in hearts that are just and true,
grant that we may be so fashioned by your grace
as to become a dwelling pleasing to you.
Through our Lord Jesus Christ, your Son,
who lives and reigns with you in the unity of the Holy Spirit,
one God, for ever and ever.

*Collect, Sixth Sunday in Ordinary Time*

# Reading (*Lectio*)

*Read the following Scripture two or three times.*

Matthew 5:20-22a, 27-28, 33-34a, 37

Jesus said to his disciples: "I tell you, unless your
righteousness surpasses that of the scribes and
Pharisees, you will not enter the kingdom of heaven.

"You have heard that it was said to your ancestors, *You
shall not kill; and whoever kills will be liable to judgment.*
But I say to you, whoever is angry with brother will be
liable to judgment.

"You have heard that it was said, *You shall not commit adultery.* But I say to you, everyone who looks at a woman with lust has already committed adultery with her in his heart.

"Again you have heard that it was said to your ancestors, *Do not take a false oath, but make good to the Lord all that you vow.* But I say to you, do not swear at all. Let your 'Yes' mean 'Yes,' and your 'No' mean 'No.' Anything more is from the evil one."

# Meditation (*Meditatio*)

*After the reading, take some time to reflect in silence on one or more of the following questions:*

- What word or words in this passage caught your attention?
- What in this passage comforted you?
- What in this passage challenged you?

*If practicing* lectio divina *as a family or in a group, after the reflection time, invite the participants to share their responses.*

# Prayer (*Oratio*)

*Read the Scripture passage one more time. Bring to the Lord the praise, petition, or thanksgiving that the Word inspires in you.*

# Contemplation (*Contemplatio*)

*Read the Scripture again, followed by this reflection:*

 What conversion of mind, heart, and life is the Lord asking of me?

 *Whoever is angry with brother will be liable to judgment.* In what circumstances am I most likely to lose my temper? What steps can I take to be kinder and more patient in my dealings with others?

*Everyone who looks at a woman with lust has already committed adultery with her in his heart.* How can avoid the temptation to treat others as objects? How can I support the dignity of every person I meet?

 *Let your "Yes" mean "Yes," and your "No" mean "No."* How often do I speak the truth in love? Can people rely upon my word?

# Closing Prayer

*After a period of silent reflection and/or discussion, all recite the Lord's Prayer and the following:*

Blessed are they whose way is blameless,
who walk in the law of the LORD.
Blessed are they who observe his decrees,
who seek him with all their heart.

You have commanded that your precepts
be diligently kept.

Oh, that I might be firm in the ways
of keeping your statutes!

Be good to your servant, that I may live
and keep your words.
Open my eyes, that I may consider
the wonders of your law.

Instruct me, O Lord, in the way of your statutes,
that I may exactly observe them.
Give me discernment, that I may observe your law
and keep it with all my heart.

*From Psalm 119*

# Living the Word This Week

*How can I make my life a gift for others in charity?*

Seek forgiveness from someone you have hurt.

# February 23, 2020

*Lectio Divina* for the Seventh Week in Ordinary Time

*We begin our prayer:*
In the name of the Father, and of the Son, and of the Holy Spirit. Amen.

Grant, we pray, almighty God,
that, always pondering spiritual things,
we may carry out in both word and deed
that which is pleasing to you.
Through our Lord Jesus Christ, your Son,
who lives and reigns with you in the unity of the Holy Spirit,
one God, for ever and ever.

*Collect, Seventh Sunday in Ordinary Time*

# Reading (*Lectio*)

*Read the following Scripture two or three times.*

Matthew 5:38-48

Jesus said to his disciples: "You have heard that it was said, *An eye for an eye and a tooth for a tooth.* But I say to you, offer no resistance to one who is evil. When someone strikes you on your right cheek, turn the other one as well. If anyone wants to go to law with you over your tunic, hand over your cloak as well. Should anyone press you into service for one mile, go for two miles. Give to the one who asks of you, and do not turn your back on one who wants to borrow.

"You have heard that it was said, *You shall love your neighbor and hate your enemy.* But I say to you, love your enemies and pray for those who persecute you, that you may be children of your heavenly Father, for he makes his sun rise on the bad and the good, and causes rain to fall on the just and the unjust. For if you love those who love you, what recompense will you have? Do not the tax collectors do the same? And if you greet your brothers only, what is unusual about that?

Do not the pagans do the same? So be perfect, just as your heavenly Father is perfect."

# Meditation (*Meditatio*)

*After the reading, take some time to reflect in silence on one or more of the following questions:*

- What word or words in this passage caught your attention?
- What in this passage comforted you?
- What in this passage challenged you?

*If practicing* lectio divina *as a family or in a group, after the reflection time, invite the participants to share their responses.*

# Prayer (*Oratio*)

*Read the Scripture passage one more time. Bring to the Lord the praise, petition, or thanksgiving that the Word inspires in you.*

# Contemplation (*Contemplatio*)

*Read the Scripture again, followed by this reflection:*

 What conversion of mind, heart, and life is the Lord asking of me?

 *When someone strikes you on your right cheek, turn the other one as well.* How do I respond when someone has hurt me? How can I be more forgiving?

 *Give to the one who asks of you, and do not turn your back on one who wants to borrow.* Am I generous with my time and resources? How do I affirm the dignity of those who are vulnerable?

*Love your enemies and pray for those who persecute you.* Who are my enemies? How do I treat them?

# Closing Prayer

*After a period of silent reflection and/or discussion, all recite the Lord's Prayer and the following:*

Bless the LORD, O my soul;
    and all my being, bless his holy name.
Bless the LORD, O my soul,
    and forget not all his benefits.

He pardons all your iniquities,
    heals all your ills.
He redeems your life from destruction,
    crowns you with kindness and compassion.

Merciful and gracious is the LORD,
    slow to anger and abounding in kindness.
Not according to our sins does he deal with us,
    nor does he requite us according to our crimes.

As far as the east is from the west,
    so far has he put our transgressions from us.
As a father has compassion on his children,
    so the LORD has compassion on those who fear him.

*From Psalm 103*

# Living the Word This Week

*How can I make my life a gift for others in charity?*

Learn more about being a Christian steward: *www.usccb.org/ beliefs-and-teachings/what-we-believe/stewardship/index.cfm.*

# February 26, 2020

*Lectio Divina* for Ash Wednesday

*We begin our prayer:*
In the name of the Father, and of the Son, and of the Holy Spirit. Amen.

Prompt our actions with your inspiration, we pray, O Lord,
and further them with your constant help,
that all we do may always begin from you
and by you be brought to completion.
Through our Lord Jesus Christ, your Son,
who lives and reigns with you in the unity of the Holy Spirit,
one God, for ever and ever.

*Collect, Thursday after Ash Wednesday*

# Reading (*Lectio*)

*Read the following Scripture two or three times.*

Matthew 6:1-6, 16-18

Jesus said to his disciples: "Take care not to perform righteous deeds in order that people may see them; otherwise, you will have no recompense from your heavenly Father. When you give alms, do not blow a trumpet before you, as the hypocrites do in the synagogues and in the streets to win the praise of others. Amen, I say to you, they have received their reward. But when you give alms, do not let your left hand know what your right is doing, so that your almsgiving may be secret. And your Father who sees in secret will repay you.

"When you pray, do not be like the hypocrites, who love to stand and pray in the synagogues and on street corners so that others may see them. Amen, I say to you, they have received their reward. But when you pray, go to your inner room, close the door, and pray to your Father in secret. And your Father who sees in secret will repay you.

"When you fast, do not look gloomy like the hypocrites. They neglect their appearance, so that they may appear to others to be fasting. Amen, I say to you, they have received their reward. But when you fast, anoint your head and wash your face, so that you may not appear to be fasting, except to your Father who is hidden. And your Father who sees what is hidden will repay you."

# Meditation (*Meditatio*)

*After the reading, take some time to reflect in silence on one or more of the following questions:*

- What word or words in this passage caught your attention?
- What in this passage comforted you?
- What in this passage challenged you?

*If practicing* lectio divina *as a family or in a group, after the reflection time, invite the participants to share their responses.*

# Prayer (*Oratio*)

*Read the Scripture passage one more time. Bring to the Lord the praise, petition, or thanksgiving that the Word inspires in you.*

# Contemplation (*Contemplatio*)

*Read the Scripture again, followed by this reflection:*

 What conversion of mind, heart, and life is the Lord asking of me?

 *Take care not to perform righteous deeds in order that people may see them.* Do I judge people by appearances and other external factors? How often am I willing to serve without recognition?

*They have received their reward.* What motivates me to act justly? What do I hope to gain by living a good life?

 *But when you fast, anoint your head and wash your face, so that you may not appear to be fasting, except to your Father who is hidden.* How often do I bring my best to God? What joys do I find in living according to God's will?

# Closing Prayer

*After a period of silent reflection and/or discussion, all recite the Lord's Prayer and the following:*

Have mercy on me, O God, in your goodness;
    in the greatness of your compassion wipe out my offense.
Thoroughly wash me from my guilt
    and of my sin cleanse me.

For I acknowledge my offense,
    and my sin is before me always:

"Against you only have I sinned,
and done what is evil in your sight."

A clean heart create for me, O God,
and a steadfast spirit renew within me.
Cast me not out from your presence,
and your Holy Spirit take not from me.

Give me back the joy of your salvation,
and a willing spirit sustain in me.
O Lord, open my lips,
and my mouth shall proclaim your praise.

*From Psalm 51*

# Living the Word This Week

*How can I make my life a gift for others in charity?*

Decide on your Lenten sacrifice and/or choose an additional
spiritual practice for Lent.

# MARCH 1, 2020

*Lectio Divina* for the First Week of Lent

*We begin our prayer:*
In the name of the Father, and of the Son, and of the Holy Spirit. Amen.

Bestow on us, we pray, O Lord,
a spirit of always pondering on what is right
and of hastening to carry it out,
and, since without you we cannot exist,
may we be enabled to live according to your will.
Through our Lord Jesus Christ, your Son,
who lives and reigns with you in the unity of the Holy Spirit,
one God, for ever and ever.

*Collect, Thursday of the First Week of Lent*

# Reading (*Lectio*)

*Read the following Scripture two or three times.*

Matthew 4:1-11

At that time Jesus was led by the Spirit into the desert to be tempted by the devil. He fasted for forty days and forty nights, and afterwards he was hungry. The tempter approached and said to him, "If you are the Son of God, command that these stones become loaves of bread."

He said in reply, "It is written:

*One does not live on bread alone,*
*but on every word that comes forth from the mouth of*
*God."*

Then the devil took him to the holy city, and made him stand on the parapet of the temple, and said to him, "If you are the Son of God, throw yourself down. For it is written:

*He will command his angels concerning you*
*and with their hands they will support you,*
*lest you dash your foot against a stone."*

Jesus answered him, "Again it is written,

*You shall not put the Lord, your God, to the test."*

Then the devil took him up to a very high mountain, and showed him all the kingdoms of the world in their magnificence, and he said to him, "All these I shall give to you, if you will prostrate yourself and worship me." At this, Jesus said to him, "Get away, Satan! It is written:

*The Lord, your God, shall you worship*
*and him alone shall you serve."*

Then the devil left him and, behold, angels came and ministered to him.

# Meditation (*Meditatio*)

*After the reading, take some time to reflect in silence on one or more of the following questions:*

- What word or words in this passage caught your attention?
- What in this passage comforted you?
- What in this passage challenged you?

*If practicing* lectio divina *as a family or in a group, after the reflection time, invite the participants to share their responses.*

# Prayer (*Oratio*)

*Read the Scripture passage one more time. Bring to the Lord the praise, petition, or thanksgiving that the Word inspires in you.*

# Contemplation (*Contemplatio*)

*Read the Scripture again, followed by this reflection:*

 What conversion of mind, heart, and life is the Lord asking of me?

*He fasted for forty days and forty nights, and afterwards he was hungry.* For what do I hunger? How am I helping to address the physical and spiritual hunger of others?

 *If you are the Son of God, throw yourself down.* How do I test God's love for me? How can I grow in trust of God?

 *Behold, angels came and ministered to him.* How have I felt God's care this week? How can I share God's loving care with those in need?

# Closing Prayer

*After a period of silent reflection and/or discussion, all recite the*
*Lord's Prayer and the following:*

Have mercy on me, O God, in your goodness;
   in the greatness of your compassion wipe out my offense.
Thoroughly wash me from my guilt
   and of my sin cleanse me.

For I acknowledge my offense,
   and my sin is before me always:
"Against you only have I sinned,
   and done what is evil in your sight."

A clean heart create for me, O God,
   and a steadfast spirit renew within me.
Cast me not out from your presence,
   and your Holy Spirit take not from me.

Give me back the joy of your salvation,
   and a willing spirit sustain in me.
O Lord, open my lips,
   and my mouth shall proclaim your praise.

*From Psalm 51*

# Living the Word This Week

*How can I make my life a gift for others in charity?*

Participate in a parish effort to feed the homeless or contribute
time or money to a food pantry.

# MARCH 8, 2020

*Lectio Divina* for the Second Week of Lent

*We begin our prayer:*
In the name of the Father, and of the Son, and of the Holy Spirit. Amen.

Keep your family, O Lord,
schooled always in good works,
and so comfort them with your protection here
as to lead them graciously to gifts on high.
Through our Lord Jesus Christ, your Son,
who lives and reigns with you in the unity of the Holy Spirit,
one God, for ever and ever.

*Collect, Wednesday of the Second Week of Lent*

# Reading (*Lectio*)

*Read the following Scripture two or three times.*

Matthew 17:1-9

Jesus took Peter, James, and John his brother, and led them up a high mountain by themselves. And he was transfigured before them; his face shone like the sun and his clothes became white as light. And behold, Moses and Elijah appeared to them, conversing with him. Then Peter said to Jesus in reply, "Lord, it is good that we are here. If you wish, I will make three tents here, one for you, one for Moses, and one for Elijah."

While he was still speaking, behold, a bright cloud cast a shadow over them, then from the cloud came a voice that said, "This is my beloved Son, with whom I am well pleased; listen to him." When the disciples heard this, they fell prostrate and were very much afraid. But Jesus came and touched them, saying, "Rise, and do not be afraid."

And when the disciples raised their eyes, they saw no one else but Jesus alone.

As they were coming down from the mountain, Jesus charged them, "Do not tell the vision to anyone until the Son of Man has been raised from the dead."

# Meditation (*Meditatio*)

*After the reading, take some time to reflect in silence on one or more of the following questions:*

- What word or words in this passage caught your attention?
- What in this passage comforted you?
- What in this passage challenged you?

*If practicing* lectio divina *as a family or in a group, after the reflection time, invite the participants to share their responses.*

# Prayer (*Oratio*)

*Read the Scripture passage one more time. Bring to the Lord the praise, petition, or thanksgiving that the Word inspires in you.*

# Contemplation (*Contemplatio*)

*Read the Scripture again, followed by this reflection:*

 What conversion of mind, heart, and life is the Lord asking of me?

 *Jesus took Peter, James, and John his brother, and led them up a high mountain by themselves.* How often do I take time for quiet, solitary prayer? What distracts me from time with the Lord?

 *And behold, Moses and Elijah appeared to them, conversing with him.* Am I truthful and kind in my conversation? Do I share or hide my faith in my conversations?

*Lord, it is good that we are here.* How can I take time during the day to place myself in God's presence? Where do I feel God's presence most strongly?

# Closing Prayer

*After a period of silent reflection and/or discussion, all recite the Lord's Prayer and the following:*

Upright is the word of the LORD,
  and all his works are trustworthy.
He loves justice and right;
  of the kindness of the LORD the earth is full.

See, the eyes of the LORD are upon those who fear him,
  upon those who hope for his kindness,
To deliver them from death
  and preserve them in spite of famine.

Our soul waits for the LORD,
  who is our help and our shield.
May your kindness, O LORD, be upon us
  who have put our hope in you.

*From Psalm 33*

# Living the Word This Week

*How can I make my life a gift for others in charity?*

During the week, make a visit to a church for quiet prayer before the Blessed Sacrament or to pray the Stations of the Cross.

# MARCH 15, 2020

*Lectio Divina* for the Third Week of Lent

*We begin our prayer:*
In the name of the Father, and of the Son, and of the Holy
Spirit. Amen.

Look graciously, O Lord,
upon the faithful who implore your mercy,
that, trusting in your kindness,
they may spread far and wide
the gifts your charity has bestowed.
Through Christ our Lord.

*Prayer over the People, Friday of the Third Week of Lent*

# Reading (*Lectio*)

*Read the following Scripture two or three times.*

John 4:5-15, 19b-26, 39a, 40-42

Jesus came to a town of Samaria called Sychar, near
the plot of land that Jacob had given to his son
Joseph. Jacob's well was there. Jesus, tired from his
journey, sat down there at the well. It was about noon.

A woman of Samaria came to draw water. Jesus said to
her, "Give me a drink." His disciples had gone into the
town to buy food. The Samaritan woman said to him,
"How can you, a Jew, ask me, a Samaritan woman,

for a drink?"—For Jews use nothing in common with Samaritans.—Jesus answered and said to her, "If you knew the gift of God and who is saying to you, 'Give me a drink,' you would have asked him and he would have given you living water." The woman said to him, "Sir, you do not even have a bucket and the cistern is deep; where then can you get this living water? Are you greater than our father Jacob, who gave us this cistern and drank from it himself with his children and his flocks?" Jesus answered and said to her, "Everyone who drinks this water will be thirsty again; but whoever drinks the water I shall give will never thirst; the water I shall give will become in him a spring of water welling up to eternal life." The woman said to him, "Sir, give me this water, so that I may not be thirsty or have to keep coming here to draw water.

"I can see that you are a prophet. Our ancestors worshiped on this mountain; but you people say that the place to worship is in Jerusalem." Jesus said to her, "Believe me, woman, the hour is coming when you will worship the Father neither on this mountain nor in Jerusalem. You people worship what you do not understand; we worship what we understand, because salvation is from the Jews. But the hour is coming, and is now here, when true worshipers will worship the Father in Spirit and truth; and indeed the Father seeks such people to worship him. God is Spirit, and those who worship him must worship in Spirit and truth." The woman said to him, "I know that the Messiah is coming, the one called the Christ; when he comes, he will tell us everything." Jesus said to her, "I am he, the one who is speaking with you."

Many of the Samaritans of that town began to believe in him. When the Samaritans came to him, they invited him to stay with them; and he stayed there two days. Many more began to believe in him because of his word, and they said to the woman, "We no longer believe because of your word; for we have heard for ourselves, and we know that this is truly the savior of the world."

# Meditation (*Meditatio*)

*After the reading, take some time to reflect in silence on one or more of the following questions:*

- What word or words in this passage caught your attention?
- What in this passage comforted you?
- What in this passage challenged you?

*If practicing* lectio divina *as a family or in a group, after the reflection time, invite the participants to share their responses.*

# Prayer (*Oratio*)

*Read the Scripture passage one more time. Bring to the Lord the praise, petition, or thanksgiving that the Word inspires in you.*

# Contemplation (*Contemplatio*)

*Read the Scripture again, followed by this reflection:*

 What conversion of mind, heart, and life is the Lord asking of me?

 *Jesus, tired from his journey, sat down there at the well.* Does my daily schedule allow me time for prayer and rest? Does the way I spend my time, energy, and money reflect my priorities?

 *You would have asked him and he would have given you living water.* For what do I need to ask the Lord? How can I grow in reliance that God will provide for all my needs?

*God is Spirit, and those who worship him must worship in Spirit and truth.* Am I attentive in prayer or does my mind wander? How can I learn more about the Mass?

# Closing Prayer

*After a period of silent reflection and/or discussion, all recite the Lord's Prayer and the following:*

Come, let us sing joyfully to the LORD;
  let us acclaim the Rock of our salvation.
Let us come into his presence with thanksgiving;
  let us joyfully sing psalms to him.

Come, let us bow down in worship;
  let us kneel before the LORD who made us.
For he is our God,
  and we are the people he shepherds, the flock he guides.

Oh, that today you would hear his voice:
  "Harden not your hearts as at Meribah,
    as in the day of Massah in the desert,
Where your fathers tempted me;
  they tested me though they had seen my works."

*From Psalm 95*

# Living the Word This Week

*How can I make my life a gift for others in charity?*

Attend daily Mass at least one day this week and be very attentive to the prayers and gestures of the Mass.

# March 22, 2020

*Lectio Divina* for the Fourth Week of Lent

*We begin our prayer:*
In the name of the Father, and of the Son, and of the Holy
Spirit. Amen.

Look upon those who call to you, O Lord,
and sustain the weak;
give life by your unfailing light
to those who walk in the shadow of death,
and bring those rescued by your mercy from every evil
to reach the highest good.
Through Christ our Lord.

*Prayer over the People, Sunday of the Fourth Week of Lent*

# Reading (*Lectio*)

*Read the following Scripture two or three times.*

John 9:1, 6-9, 13-17, 34-38

As Jesus passed by he saw a man blind from birth.
He spat on the ground and made clay with the
saliva, and smeared the clay on his eyes, and said to
him, "Go wash in the Pool of Siloam"—which means
Sent—. So he went and washed, and came back able
to see.

His neighbors and those who had seen him earlier as a beggar said, "Isn't this the one who used to sit and beg?" Some said, "It is," but others said, "No, he just looks like him." He said, "I am."

They brought the one who was once blind to the Pharisees. Now Jesus had made clay and opened his eyes on a sabbath. So then the Pharisees also asked him how he was able to see.

He said to them, "He put clay on my eyes, and I washed, and now I can see." So some of the Pharisees said, "This man is not from God, because he does not keep the sabbath." But others said, "How can a sinful man do such signs?" And there was a division among them. So they said to the blind man again, "What do you have to say about him, since he opened your eyes?" He said, "He is a prophet."

They answered and said to him, "You were born totally in sin, and are you trying to teach us?" Then they threw him out.

When Jesus heard that they had thrown him out, he found him and said, "Do you believe in the Son of Man?" He answered and said, "Who is he, sir, that I may believe in him?" Jesus said to him, "You have seen him, and the one speaking with you is he." He said, "I do believe, Lord," and he worshiped him.

# Meditation (*Meditatio*)

*After the reading, take some time to reflect in silence on one or more of the following questions:*

- What word or words in this passage caught your attention?
- What in this passage comforted you?
- What in this passage challenged you?

*If practicing* lectio divina *as a family or in a group, after the reflection time, invite the participants to share their responses.*

# Prayer (*Oratio*)

*Read the Scripture passage one more time. Bring to the Lord the praise, petition, or thanksgiving that the Word inspires in you.*

# Contemplation (*Contemplatio*)

*Read the Scripture again, followed by this reflection:*

 What conversion of mind, heart, and life is the Lord asking of me?

*So he went and washed, and came back able to see.* How can I be more attentive to God's presence in my life? How can I be more attentive to the needs of those around me?

*And there was a division among them.* How do my actions add to the divisiveness present in our culture? How can I be a force for unity?

*He said, "I do believe, Lord," and he worshiped him.* How can I dedicate more time to prayer, worship, and service? How committed am I to learning more about my faith?

# Closing Prayer

*After a period of silent reflection and/or discussion, all recite the Lord's Prayer and the following:*

The LORD is my shepherd; I shall not want.
    In verdant pastures he gives me repose;
beside restful waters he leads me;
    he refreshes my soul.

He guides me in right paths
    for his name's sake.
Even though I walk in the dark valley
    I fear no evil; for you are at my side
With your rod and your staff
    that give me courage.

You spread the table before me
    in the sight of my foes;
you anoint my head with oil;
    my cup overflows.

Only goodness and kindness follow me
    all the days of my life;
and I shall dwell in the house of the LORD
    for years to come.

*From Psalm 23*

# Living the Word This Week

*How can I make my life a gift for others in charity?*

Make plans to receive the Sacrament of Penance before Lent ends.

# MARCH 29, 2020

*Lectio Divina* for the Fifth Week of Lent

*We begin our prayer:*
In the name of the Father, and of the Son, and of the Holy
Spirit. Amen.

Enlighten, O God of compassion,
the hearts of your children, sanctified by penance,
and in your kindness
grant those you stir to a sense of devotion
a gracious hearing when they cry out to you.
Through our Lord Jesus Christ, your Son,
who lives and reigns with you in the unity of the Holy Spirit,
one God, for ever and ever.

*Collect, Wednesday of the Fifth Week of Lent*

## Reading (*Lectio*)

*Read the following Scripture two or three times.*

John 11:3-7, 17, 20-27, 33b-45

The sisters of Lazarus sent word to Jesus, saying,
"Master, the one you love is ill." When Jesus heard
this he said, "This illness is not to end in death, but
is for the glory of God, that the Son of God may be
glorified through it." Now Jesus loved Martha and her
sister and Lazarus. So when he heard that he was ill,
he remained for two days in the place where he was.

Then after this he said to his disciples, "Let us go back to Judea."

When Jesus arrived, he found that Lazarus had already been in the tomb for four days. When Martha heard that Jesus was coming, she went to meet him; but Mary sat at home. Martha said to Jesus, "Lord, if you had been here, my brother would not have died. But even now I know that whatever you ask of God, God will give you." Jesus said to her, "Your brother will rise." Martha said, "I know he will rise, in the resurrection on the last day." Jesus told her, "I am the resurrection and the life; whoever believes in me, even if he dies, will live, and everyone who lives and believes in me will never die. Do you believe this?" She said to him, "Yes, Lord. I have come to believe that you are the Christ, the Son of God, the one who is coming into the world."

He became perturbed and deeply troubled, and said, "Where have you laid him?" They said to him, "Sir, come and see." And Jesus wept. So the Jews said, "See how he loved him." But some of them said, "Could not the one who opened the eyes of the blind man have done something so that this man would not have died?"

So Jesus, perturbed again, came to the tomb. It was a cave, and a stone lay across it. Jesus said, "Take away the stone." Martha, the dead man's sister, said to him, "Lord, by now there will be a stench; he has been dead for four days." Jesus said to her, "Did I not tell you that if you believe you will see the glory of God?" So they took away the stone. And Jesus raised his eyes and said, "Father, I thank you for hearing me. I know that you always hear me; but because of the crowd here I have said this, that they may believe that you sent me." And when he had said this, He cried out in a loud voice, "Lazarus, come out!" The dead man came out, tied hand and foot with burial bands, and his face was wrapped in a cloth. So Jesus said to them, "Untie him and let him go."

Now many of the Jews who had come to Mary and seen what he had done began to believe in him.

# Meditation (*Meditatio*)

*After the reading, take some time to reflect in silence on one or more of the following questions:*

- What word or words in this passage caught your attention?
- What in this passage comforted you?
- What in this passage challenged you?

*If practicing* lectio divina *as a family or in a group, after the reflection time, invite the participants to share their responses.*

# Prayer (*Oratio*)

*Read the Scripture passage one more time. Bring to the Lord the praise, petition, or thanksgiving that the Word inspires in you.*

# Contemplation (*Contemplatio*)

*Read the Scripture again, followed by this reflection:*

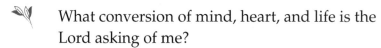 What conversion of mind, heart, and life is the Lord asking of me?

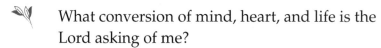 *When Martha heard that Jesus was coming, she went to meet him.* Where do I meet Jesus? How can I make spending time with the Lord a priority?

 *But even now I know that whatever you ask of God, God will give you.* What do I need to ask God for this week? How can I be more open to God's will in my life?

*I have come to believe that you are the Christ, the Son of God, the one who is coming into the world.* What strengthens my faith? What resources in my parish and diocese will help me learn more about what the Church believes?

# Closing Prayer

*After a period of silent reflection and/or discussion, all recite the Lord's Prayer and the following:*

Out of the depths I cry to you, O LORD;
  LORD, hear my voice!
Let your ears be attentive
  to my voice in supplication.

If you, O LORD, mark iniquities,
  LORD, who can stand?
But with you is forgiveness,
  that you may be revered.

I trust in the LORD;
  my soul trusts in his word.
More than sentinels wait for the dawn,
let Israel wait for the LORD.

For with the LORD is kindness
  and with him is plenteous redemption;

And he will redeem Israel
from all their iniquities.

*From Psalm 130*

## Living the Word This Week

*How can I make my life a gift for others in charity?*

Send a note or make a visit to someone who is ill or grieving.

# APRIL 5, 2020

*Lectio Divina* for Holy Week

*We begin our prayer:*
In the name of the Father, and of the Son, and of the Holy
Spirit. Amen.

O God, who willed your Son to submit for our sake
to the yoke of the Cross,
so that you might drive from us the power of the enemy,
grant us, your servants, to attain the grace of the resurrection.
Through our Lord Jesus Christ, your Son,
who lives and reigns with you in the unity of the Holy Spirit,
one God, for ever and ever.

*Collect, Wednesday of Holy Week*

# Reading (*Lectio*)

*Read the following Scripture two or three times.*

Matthew 21:1-11

When Jesus and the disciples drew near Jerusalem
and came to Bethphage on the Mount of Olives,
Jesus sent two disciples, saying to them, "Go into the
village opposite you, and immediately you will find an
ass tethered, and a colt with her. Untie them and bring
them here to me. And if anyone should say anything to
you, reply, 'The master has need of them.' Then he will
send them at once." This happened so that what had

been spoken through the prophet might be fulfilled:

*Say to daughter Zion,*
*"Behold, your king comes to you,*
*    meek and riding on an ass,*
*    and on a colt, the foal of a beast of burden."*

The disciples went and did as Jesus had ordered them.
They brought the ass and the colt and laid their cloaks
over them, and he sat upon them. The very large
crowd spread their cloaks on the road, while others cut
branches from the trees and strewed them on the road.
The crowds preceding him and those following kept
crying out and saying:

"Hosanna to the Son of David;
    blessed is he who comes in the name of the Lord;
hosanna in the highest."

And when he entered Jerusalem the whole city was
shaken and asked, "Who is this?" And the crowds
replied, "This is Jesus the prophet, from Nazareth
in Galilee."

# Meditation (*Meditatio*)

*After the reading, take some time to reflect in silence on one or more*
*of the following questions:*

- What word or words in this passage caught
  your attention?
- What in this passage comforted you?
- What in this passage challenged you?

*If practicing* lectio divina *as a family or in a group, after the*
*reflection time, invite the participants to share their responses.*

# Prayer (*Oratio*)

*Read the Scripture passage one more time. Bring to the Lord the praise, petition, or thanksgiving that the Word inspires in you.*

# Contemplation (*Contemplatio*)

*Read the Scripture again, followed by this reflection:*

 What conversion of mind, heart, and life is the Lord asking of me?

 *The master has need of them.* What does Jesus want from me? What stands in the way of my giving myself to the Lord?

*The disciples went and did as Jesus had ordered them.* How well does my way of living match what I believe? How can I follow the Lord's commands with greater willingness and joy?

 *And when he entered Jerusalem the whole city was shaken.* What part of Jesus' message challenges me most deeply? What parts of Jesus' message give me the most comfort?

# Closing Prayer

*After a period of silent reflection and/or discussion, all recite the Lord's Prayer and the following:*

All who see me scoff at me;
    they mock me with parted lips, they wag their heads:
"He relied on the Lord; let him deliver him,
    let him rescue him, if he loves him."

Indeed, many dogs surround me,
    a pack of evildoers closes in upon me;

They have pierced my hands and my feet;
  I can count all my bones.

They divide my garments among them,
  and for my vesture they cast lots.
But you, O LORD, be not far from me;
  O my help, hasten to aid me.

I will proclaim your name to my brethren;
  in the midst of the assembly I will praise you:
"You who fear the LORD, praise him;
  all you descendants of Jacob, give glory to him;
  revere him, all you descendants of Israel!"

*From Psalm 22*

# Living the Word This Week

*How can I make my life a gift for others in charity?*

Plan to attend the Paschal Triduum services in your parish and meditate on the saving death and resurrection of Jesus Christ.

# APRIL 12, 2020

*Lectio Divina* for the Octave of Easter

*We begin our prayer:*
In the name of the Father, and of the Son, and of the Holy
Spirit. Amen.

O God, who have united the many nations
in confessing your name,
grant that those reborn in the font of Baptism
may be one in the faith of their hearts
and the homage of their deeds.
Through our Lord Jesus Christ, your Son,
who lives and reigns with you in the unity of the Holy Spirit,
one God, for ever and ever.

*Collect, Thursday within the Octave of Easter*

# Reading (*Lectio*)

*Read the following Scripture two or three times.*

Matthew 28:1-10

After the sabbath, as the first day of the week was
dawning, Mary Magdalene and the other Mary
came to see the tomb. And behold, there was a great
earthquake; for an angel of the Lord descended from
heaven, approached, rolled back the stone, and sat
upon it. His appearance was like lightning and his
clothing was white as snow. The guards were shaken

with fear of him and became like dead men. Then the angel said to the women in reply, "Do not be afraid! I know that you are seeking Jesus the crucified. He is not here, for he has been raised just as he said. Come and see the place where he lay. Then go quickly and tell his disciples, 'He has been raised from the dead, and he is going before you to Galilee; there you will see him.' Behold, I have told you." Then they went away quickly from the tomb, fearful yet overjoyed, and ran to announce this to his disciples. And behold, Jesus met them on their way and greeted them. They approached, embraced his feet, and did him homage. Then Jesus said to them, "Do not be afraid. Go tell my brothers to go to Galilee, and there they will see me."

# Meditation (*Meditatio*)

*After the reading, take some time to reflect in silence on one or more of the following questions:*

- What word or words in this passage caught your attention?
- What in this passage comforted you?
- What in this passage challenged you?

*If practicing* lectio divina *as a family or in a group, after the reflection time, invite the participants to share their responses.*

# Prayer (*Oratio*)

*Read the Scripture passage one more time. Bring to the Lord the praise, petition, or thanksgiving that the Word inspires in you.*

# Contemplation (*Contemplatio*)

*Read the Scripture again, followed by this reflection:*

 What conversion of mind, heart, and life is the Lord asking of me?

 *I know that you are seeking Jesus the crucified. He is not here, for he has been raised just as he said.* How confident am I in my faith? What encourages me in times of doubt?

 *Then they went away quickly from the tomb, fearful yet overjoyed, and ran to announce this to his disciples.* What fears and concerns keep me from sharing my faith? When have I found great joy in sharing my faith?

*They approached, embraced his feet, and did him homage.* How do I show my love for God? How can I grow closer to Jesus?

# Closing Prayer

*After a period of silent reflection and/or discussion, all recite the Lord's Prayer and the following:*

Give thanks to the LORD, for he is good,
   for his mercy endures forever.
Let the house of Israel say,
   "His mercy endures forever."

"The right hand of the LORD has struck with power;
   the right hand of the LORD is exalted.
I shall not die, but live,
   and declare the works of the LORD."

The stone which the builders rejected
   has become the cornerstone.
By the LORD has this been done;
   it is wonderful in our eyes.

*From Psalm 118*

# Living the Word This Week

*How can I make my life a gift for others in charity?*

Read *Laudato Si'* on care for the environment: *http:// w2.vatican.va/content/francesco/en/encyclicals/documents/papa-francesco_20150524_enciclica-laudato-si.html.*

# April 19, 2020

*Lectio Divina* for the Second Week of Easter

*We begin our prayer:*
In the name of the Father, and of the Son, and of the Holy Spirit. Amen.

O God, who willed that through the paschal mysteries
the gates of mercy should stand open for your faithful,
look upon us and have mercy,
that as we follow, by your gift, the way you desire for us,
so may we never stray from the paths of life.
Through our Lord Jesus Christ, your Son,
who lives and reigns with you in the unity of the Holy Spirit,
one God, for ever and ever.

*Collect, Saturday of the Second Week of Easter*

# Reading (*Lectio*)

*Read the following Scripture two or three times.*

John 20:19-31

On the evening of that first day of the week, when the doors were locked, where the disciples were, for fear of the Jews, Jesus came and stood in their midst and said to them, "Peace be with you." When he had said this, he showed them his hands and his side. The disciples rejoiced when they saw the Lord. Jesus said to them again, "Peace be with you. As the Father has sent me, so I send you." And when he had said this, he breathed on them and said to them, "Receive the Holy Spirit. Whose sins you forgive are forgiven them, and whose sins you retain are retained."

Thomas, called Didymus, one of the Twelve, was not with them when Jesus came. So the other disciples said to him, "We have seen the Lord." But he said to them, "Unless I see the mark of the nails in his hands and put my finger into the nailmarks and put my hand into his side, I will not believe."

Now a week later his disciples were again inside and Thomas was with them. Jesus came, although the doors were locked, and stood in their midst and said, "Peace be with you." Then he said to Thomas, "Put your finger here and see my hands, and bring your hand and put it into my side, and do not be unbelieving, but believe." Thomas answered and said to him, "My Lord and my God!" Jesus said to him, "Have you come to believe because you have seen me? Blessed are those who have not seen and have believed."

Now, Jesus did many other signs in the presence of his disciples that are not written in this book. But these are written that you may come to believe that Jesus is the Christ, the Son of God, and that through this belief you may have life in his name.

# Meditation (*Meditatio*)

*After the reading, take some time to reflect in silence on one or more of the following questions:*

- What word or words in this passage caught your attention?
- What in this passage comforted you?
- What in this passage challenged you?

*If practicing* lectio divina *as a family or in a group, after the reflection time, invite the participants to share their responses.*

# Prayer (*Oratio*)

*Read the Scripture passage one more time. Bring to the Lord the praise, petition, or thanksgiving that the Word inspires in you.*

# Contemplation (*Contemplatio*)

*Read the Scripture again, followed by this reflection:*

 What conversion of mind, heart, and life is the Lord asking of me?

 *On the evening of that first day of the week, when the doors were locked . . . for fear.* What fears keep me

from living my faith more fully? Whom have I
locked out of my life because of fear?

 *Unless I see the mark of the nails in his hands and put
my finger into the nailmarks and put my hand into
his side, I will not believe.* What are the obstacles
to my belief? How can I help others overcome
their doubts?

 *Blessed are those who have not seen and have believed.*
How is my faith a blessing to me and my family?
How can I accompany those who are skeptical?

# Closing Prayer

*After a period of silent reflection and/or discussion, all recite the
Lord's Prayer and the following:*

Let the house of Israel say,
   "His mercy endures forever."
Let the house of Aaron say,
   "His mercy endures forever."
Let those who fear the LORD say,
   "His mercy endures forever."

I was hard pressed and was falling,
   but the LORD helped me.
My strength and my courage is the LORD,
   and he has been my savior.
The joyful shout of victory
   in the tents of the just:

The stone which the builders rejected
   has become the cornerstone.
By the LORD has this been done;
   it is wonderful in our eyes.
This is the day the LORD has made;
   let us be glad and rejoice in it.

*From Psalm 118*

# Living the Word This Week

*How can I make my life a gift for others in charity?*

Participate in justice and peace initiatives sponsored by the
parish or diocese.

# April 26, 2020

*Lectio Divina* for the Third Week of Easter

*We begin our prayer:*
In the name of the Father, and of the Son, and of the Holy
Spirit. Amen.

Almighty ever-living God,
let us feel your compassion more readily
during these days when, by your gift,
we have known it more fully,
so that those you have freed from the darkness of error
may cling more firmly to the teachings of your truth.
Through our Lord Jesus Christ, your Son,
who lives and reigns with you in the unity of the Holy Spirit,
one God, for ever and ever.

*Collect, Thursday of the Third Week of Easter*

# Reading (*Lectio*)

*Read the following Scripture two or three times.*

Luke 24:13-35

That very day, the first day of the week, two of
Jesus' disciples were going to a village seven
miles from Jerusalem called Emmaus, and they were
conversing about all the things that had occurred.
And it happened that while they were conversing and
debating, Jesus himself drew near and walked with

them, but their eyes were prevented from recognizing him. He asked them, "What are you discussing as you walk along?" They stopped, looking downcast. One of them, named Cleopas, said to him in reply, "Are you the only visitor to Jerusalem who does not know of the things that have taken place there in these days?" And he replied to them, "What sort of things?" They said to him, "The things that happened to Jesus the Nazarene, who was a prophet mighty in deed and word before God and all the people, how our chief priests and rulers both handed him over to a sentence of death and crucified him. But we were hoping that he would be the one to redeem Israel; and besides all this, it is now the third day since this took place. Some women from our group, however, have astounded us: they were at the tomb early in the morning and did not find his body; they came back and reported that they had indeed seen a vision of angels who announced that he was alive. Then some of those with us went to the tomb and found things just as the women had described, but him they did not see." And he said to them, "Oh, how foolish you are! How slow of heart to believe all that the prophets spoke! Was it not necessary that the Christ should suffer these things and enter into his glory?" Then beginning with Moses and all the prophets, he interpreted to them what referred to him in all the Scriptures. As they approached the village to which they were going, he gave the impression that he was going on farther. But they urged him, "Stay with us, for it is nearly evening and the day is almost over." So he went in to stay with them. And it happened that, while he was with them at table, he took bread, said the blessing, broke it, and gave it to them. With that their eyes were opened and they recognized him, but he vanished from their sight. Then they said to each other, "Were not our hearts burning within us while he spoke to us on the way and opened the Scriptures to us?" So they set out at once and returned to Jerusalem where they found gathered together the eleven and those with them who were saying, "The Lord has truly been raised and has appeared to Simon!" Then the two recounted what had taken place on the way and how he was made known to them in the breaking of bread.

# Meditation (*Meditatio*)

*After the reading, take some time to reflect in silence on one or more of the following questions:*

- What word or words in this passage caught your attention?
- What in this passage comforted you?
- What in this passage challenged you?

*If practicing* lectio divina *as a family or in a group, after the reflection time, invite the participants to share their responses.*

# Prayer (*Oratio*)

*Read the Scripture passage one more time. Bring to the Lord the praise, petition, or thanksgiving that the Word inspires in you.*

# Contemplation (*Contemplatio*)

*Read the Scripture again, followed by this reflection:*

 What conversion of mind, heart, and life is the Lord asking of me?

 *Jesus himself drew near and walked with them, but their eyes were prevented from recognizing him.* Where is Jesus present that I often fail to recognize him? What keeps me from recognizing Jesus?

 *Was it not necessary that the Christ should suffer these things and enter into his glory?* What crosses am I being called to bear patiently? For what can I offer the suffering in my life?

*Were not our hearts burning within us while he spoke to us on the way and opened the Scriptures to us?* What about my faith excites me so much that I want to share it? How do I hear Jesus speaking to me?

# Closing Prayer

*After a period of silent reflection and/or discussion, all recite the Lord's Prayer and the following:*

Keep me, O God, for in you I take refuge;
    I say to the LORD, "My Lord are you."
O LORD, my allotted portion and my cup,
    you it is who hold fast my lot.

I bless the LORD who counsels me;
    even in the night my heart exhorts me.
I set the LORD ever before me;
    with him at my right hand I shall not be disturbed.

Therefore my heart is glad and my soul rejoices,
        my body, too, abides in confidence;
because you will not abandon my soul to the netherworld,
    nor will you suffer your faithful one to undergo
        corruption.

You will show me the path to life,
   abounding joy in your presence,
   the delights at your right hand forever.

*From Psalm 16*

# Living the Word This Week

*How can I make my life a gift for others in charity?*

Spend an hour this week reading Scripture.

# May 3, 2020

*Lectio Divina* for the Fourth Week of Easter

*We begin our prayer:*
In the name of the Father, and of the Son, and of the Holy
Spirit. Amen.

Almighty ever-living God,
lead us to a share in the joys of heaven,
so that the humble flock may reach
where the brave Shepherd has gone before.
Who lives and reigns with you in the unity of the Holy Spirit,
one God, for ever and ever.

*Collect, Fourth Sunday of Easter*

# Reading (*Lectio*)

*Read the following Scripture two or three times.*

John 10:1-10

Jesus said: "Amen, amen, I say to you, whoever does
not enter a sheepfold through the gate but climbs
over elsewhere is a thief and a robber. But whoever
enters through the gate is the shepherd of the sheep.
The gatekeeper opens it for him, and the sheep hear
his voice, as the shepherd calls his own sheep by
name and leads them out. When he has driven out
all his own, he walks ahead of them, and the sheep
follow him, because they recognize his voice. But

they will not follow a stranger; they will run away from him, because they do not recognize the voice of strangers." Although Jesus used this figure of speech, the Pharisees did not realize what he was trying to tell them.

So Jesus said again, "Amen, amen, I say to you, I am the gate for the sheep. All who came before me are thieves and robbers, but the sheep did not listen to them. I am the gate. Whoever enters through me will be saved, and will come in and go out and find pasture. A thief comes only to steal and slaughter and destroy; I came so that they might have life and have it more abundantly."

# Meditation (*Meditatio*)

*After the reading, take some time to reflect in silence on one or more of the following questions:*

- What word or words in this passage caught your attention?
- What in this passage comforted you?
- What in this passage challenged you?

*If practicing* lectio divina *as a family or in a group, after the reflection time, invite the participants to share their responses.*

# Prayer (*Oratio*)

*Read the Scripture passage one more time. Bring to the Lord the praise, petition, or thanksgiving that the Word inspires in you.*

# Contemplation (*Contemplatio*)

*Read the Scripture again, followed by this reflection:*

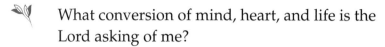 What conversion of mind, heart, and life is the Lord asking of me?

*The shepherd calls his own sheep by name and leads them out.* How can I discern God's call for me? What is God leading me to do?

*But they will not follow a stranger; they will run away from him, because they do not recognize the voice of strangers.* What voices call me away from Christ? What temptations do I need to run away from?

*I came so that they might have life and have it more abundantly.* When do I feel most alive? What can draw me closer to God in those moments?

# Closing Prayer

*After a period of silent reflection and/or discussion, all recite the Lord's Prayer and the following:*

The LORD is my shepherd; I shall not want.
>In verdant pastures he gives me repose;
beside restful waters he leads me;
>he refreshes my soul.

He guides me in right paths
>for his name's sake.
Even though I walk in the dark valley
>I fear no evil; for you are at my side.
With your rod and your staff
>that give me courage.

You spread the table before me
>in the sight of my foes;
you anoint my head with oil;
>my cup overflows.

Only goodness and kindness follow me
    all the days of my life;
and I shall dwell in the house of the LORD
    for years to come.

*From Psalm 23*

# Living the Word This Week

*How can I make my life a gift for others in charity?*

Pray for those discerning a vocation to the priesthood, the consecrated life, or the permanent diaconate.

# May 10, 2020

*Lectio Divina* for the Fifth Week of Easter

*We begin our prayer:*
In the name of the Father, and of the Son, and of the Holy
Spirit. Amen.

O God, who restore us to eternal life
in the Resurrection of Christ,
grant your people constancy in faith and hope,
that we may never doubt the promises
of which we have learned from you.
Through our Lord Jesus Christ, your Son,
who lives and reigns with you in the unity of the Holy Spirit,
one God, for ever and ever.

*Collect, Tuesday of the Fifth Week of Easter*

# Reading (*Lectio*)

*Read the following Scripture two or three times.*

John 14:1-12

Jesus said to his disciples: "Do not let your hearts
be troubled. You have faith in God; have faith also
in me. In my Father's house there are many dwelling
places. If there were not, would I have told you that I
am going to prepare a place for you? And if I go and
prepare a place for you, I will come back again and
take you to myself, so that where I am you also may

be. Where I am going you know the way." Thomas said to him, "Master, we do not know where you are going; how can we know the way?" Jesus said to him, "I am the way and the truth and the life. No one comes to the Father except through me. If you know me, then you will also know my Father. From now on you do know him and have seen him." Philip said to him, "Master, show us the Father, and that will be enough for us." Jesus said to him, "Have I been with you for so long a time and you still do not know me, Philip? Whoever has seen me has seen the Father. How can you say, 'Show us the Father'? Do you not believe that I am in the Father and the Father is in me? The words that I speak to you I do not speak on my own. The Father who dwells in me is doing his works. Believe me that I am in the Father and the Father is in me, or else, believe because of the works themselves. Amen, amen, I say to you, whoever believes in me will do the works that I do, and will do greater ones than these, because I am going to the Father."

# Meditation (*Meditatio*)

*After the reading, take some time to reflect in silence on one or more of the following questions:*

- What word or words in this passage caught your attention?
- What in this passage comforted you?
- What in this passage challenged you?

*If practicing* lectio divina *as a family or in a group, after the reflection time, invite the participants to share their responses.*

# Prayer (*Oratio*)

*Read the Scripture passage one more time. Bring to the Lord the praise, petition, or thanksgiving that the Word inspires in you.*

# Contemplation (*Contemplatio*)

*Read the Scripture again, followed by this reflection:*

 What conversion of mind, heart, and life is the Lord asking of me?

 *Do not let your hearts be troubled.* What events and situations in the world are troubling to me? How can I be a force for calm and peace?

 *In my Father's house there are many dwelling places.* Where do I feel the presence of God most strongly? Where do I pray most often?

*I am the way and the truth and the life. No one comes to the Father except through me.* Do I share the truth in all my interactions—in speech, writing, and on social media? Do I help lead others to God through word and action?

# Closing Prayer

*After a period of silent reflection and/or discussion, all recite the Lord's Prayer and the following:*

Exult, you just, in the LORD;
    praise from the upright is fitting.
Give thanks to the LORD on the harp;
    with the ten-stringed lyre chant his praises.

Upright is the word of the LORD,
    and all his works are trustworthy.
He loves justice and right;
    of the kindness of the LORD the earth is full.

See, the eyes of the LORD are upon those who fear him,
    upon those who hope for his kindness,
To deliver them from death
    and preserve them in spite of famine.

*From Psalm 33*

# Living the Word This Week

*How can I make my life a gift for others in charity?*

Learn more about the truths of the Catholic faith by reading the *United States Catholic Catechism for Adults: http://ccc.usccb. org/flipbooks/uscca/.*

# MAY 17, 2020

*Lectio Divina* for the Sixth Week of Easter

*We begin our prayer:*
In the name of the Father, and of the Son, and of the Holy
Spirit. Amen.

Hear our prayers, O Lord,
so that what was promised
by the sanctifying power of your Word
may everywhere be accomplished
through the working of the Gospel
and that all your adopted children may attain
what the testimony of truth has foretold.
Through our Lord Jesus Christ, your Son,
who lives and reigns with you in the unity of the Holy Spirit,
one God, for ever and ever.

*Collect, Friday of the Sixth Week of Easter*

# Reading (*Lectio*)

*Read the following Scripture two or three times.*

John 14:15-21

Jesus said to his disciples: "If you love me, you will
keep my commandments. And I will ask the Father,
and he will give you another Advocate to be with you
always, the Spirit of truth, whom the world cannot
accept, because it neither sees nor knows him. But you

know him, because he remains with you, and will be in you. I will not leave you orphans; I will come to you. In a little while the world will no longer see me, but you will see me, because I live and you will live. On that day you will realize that I am in my Father and you are in me and I in you. Whoever has my commandments and observes them is the one who loves me. And whoever loves me will be loved by my Father, and I will love him and reveal myself to him."

# Meditation (*Meditatio*)

*After the reading, take some time to reflect in silence on one or more of the following questions:*

- What word or words in this passage caught your attention?
- What in this passage comforted you?
- What in this passage challenged you?

*If practicing* lectio divina *as a family or in a group, after the reflection time, invite the participants to share their responses.*

# Prayer (*Oratio*)

*Read the Scripture passage one more time. Bring to the Lord the praise, petition, or thanksgiving that the Word inspires in you.*

# Contemplation (*Contemplatio*)

*Read the Scripture again, followed by this reflection:*

 What conversion of mind, heart, and life is the Lord asking of me?

 *If you love me, you will keep my commandments.* What commandments do I struggle to keep? How can I avoid temptations to disobey God's commandments?

 *I will not leave you orphans; I will come to you.* When have I felt abandoned or lost? What has strengthened and comforted me in those times?

*In a little while the world will no longer see me, but you will see me, because I live and you will live.*
Where do I see God present and active in the world? How can I help others see God?

# Closing Prayer

*After a period of silent reflection and/or discussion, all recite the Lord's Prayer and the following:*

Shout joyfully to God, all the earth,
    sing praise to the glory of his name;
    proclaim his glorious praise.
Say to God, "How tremendous are your deeds!"

"Let all on earth worship and sing praise to you,
    sing praise to your name!"
Come and see the works of God,
    his tremendous deeds among the children of Adam.

He has changed the sea into dry land;
    through the river they passed on foot;
    therefore let us rejoice in him.
He rules by his might forever.

Hear now, all you who fear God, while I declare
    what he has done for me.

Blessed be God who refused me not
my prayer or his kindness!

*From Psalm 66*

## Living the Word This Week

*How can I make my life a gift for others in charity?*

Read what the *Catechism of the Catholic Church* has to say about the Ten Commandments: *http://ccc.usccb.org/flipbooks/catechism/index.html#498.*

# MAY 21 OR MAY 24, 2020
*Lectio Divina* for the Solemnity of the Ascension

*We begin our prayer:*
In the name of the Father, and of the Son, and of the Holy
Spirit. Amen.

Gladden us with holy joys, almighty God,
and make us rejoice with devout thanksgiving,
for the Ascension of Christ your Son
is our exaltation,
and, where the Head has gone before in glory,
the Body is called to follow in hope.
Through our Lord Jesus Christ, your Son,
who lives and reigns with you in the unity of the Holy Spirit,
one God, for ever and ever.

*Collect, Ascension, Mass during the Day*

# Reading (*Lectio*)

*Read the following Scripture two or three times.*

Matthew 28:16-20

The eleven disciples went to Galilee, to the mountain
to which Jesus had ordered them. When they saw
him, they worshiped, but they doubted. Then Jesus
approached and said to them, "All power in heaven
and on earth has been given to me. Go, therefore,
and make disciples of all nations, baptizing them in

the name of the Father, and of the Son, and of the
Holy Spirit, teaching them to observe all that I have
commanded you. And behold, I am with you always,
until the end of the age."

# Meditation (*Meditatio*)

*After the reading, take some time to reflect in silence on one or more
of the following questions:*

- What word or words in this passage caught
  your attention?
- What in this passage comforted you?
- What in this passage challenged you?

*If practicing* lectio divina *as a family or in a group, after the
reflection time, invite the participants to share their responses.*

# Prayer (*Oratio*)

*Read the Scripture passage one more time. Bring to the Lord the
praise, petition, or thanksgiving that the Word inspires in you.*

# Contemplation (*Contemplatio*)

*Read the Scripture again, followed by this reflection:*

 What conversion of mind, heart, and life is the
Lord asking of me?

*When they saw him, they worshiped, but they doubted.* What distracts me from prayer and worship? How do I deal with distractions and doubts?

*All power in heaven and on earth has been given to me.* How have I seen God's power active in my life? How can I learn to surrender my will to God?

*And behold, I am with you always, until the end of the age.* How can I accompany those who are doubting or troubled? When have I invited others to experience God's presence?

# Closing Prayer

*After a period of silent reflection and/or discussion, all recite the Lord's Prayer and the following:*

All you peoples, clap your hands,
   shout to God with cries of gladness,
For the LORD, the Most High, the awesome,
   is the great king over all the earth.

God mounts his throne amid shouts of joy;
   the LORD, amid trumpet blasts.
Sing praise to God, sing praise;
   sing praise to our king, sing praise.

For king of all the earth is God;
   sing hymns of praise.
God reigns over the nations,
   God sits upon his holy throne.

*From Psalm 47*

# Living the Word This Week

*How can I make my life a gift for others in charity?*

Consider becoming involved in the RCIA (Rite of Christian Initiation of Adults) process as a catechist, sponsor, or catechumen!

# MAY 24, 2020

*Lectio Divina* for the Seventh Week of Easter

*We begin our prayer:*
In the name of the Father, and of the Son, and of the Holy
Spirit. Amen.

Grant, we pray, almighty and merciful God,
that the Holy Spirit, coming near
and dwelling graciously within us,
may make of us a perfect temple of his glory.
Through our Lord Jesus Christ, your Son,
who lives and reigns with you in the unity of the Holy Spirit,
one God, for ever and ever.

*Collect, Tuesday of the Seventh Week of Easter*

# Reading (*Lectio*)

*Read the following Scripture two or three times.*

John 17:1-11a

Jesus raised his eyes to heaven and said, "Father, the
hour has come. Give glory to your son, so that your
son may glorify you, just as you gave him authority
over all people, so that your son may give eternal life
to all you gave him. Now this is eternal life, that they
should know you, the only true God, and the one
whom you sent, Jesus Christ. I glorified you on earth
by accomplishing the work that you gave me to do.

Now glorify me, Father, with you, with the glory that I had with you before the world began.

"I revealed your name to those whom you gave me out of the world. They belonged to you, and you gave them to me, and they have kept your word. Now they know that everything you gave me is from you, because the words you gave to me I have given to them, and they accepted them and truly understood that I came from you, and they have believed that you sent me. I pray for them. I do not pray for the world but for the ones you have given me, because they are yours, and everything of mine is yours and everything of yours is mine, and I have been glorified in them. And now I will no longer be in the world, but they are in the world, while I am coming to you."

# Meditation (*Meditatio*)

*After the reading, take some time to reflect in silence on one or more of the following questions:*

- What word or words in this passage caught your attention?
- What in this passage comforted you?
- What in this passage challenged you?

*If practicing* lectio divina *as a family or in a group, after the reflection time, invite the participants to share their responses.*

# Prayer (*Oratio*)

*Read the Scripture passage one more time. Bring to the Lord the praise, petition, or thanksgiving that the Word inspires in you.*

# Contemplation (*Contemplatio*)

*Read the Scripture again, followed by this reflection:*

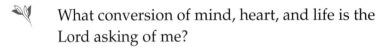 What conversion of mind, heart, and life is the Lord asking of me?

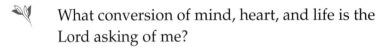 *You gave him authority over all people.* How do I interact with those who have authority over me? How do I treat those under my authority?

 *I revealed your name to those whom you gave me out of the world.* How do I show reverence for Jesus' name? How do I share my values when the prevailing culture does not affirm them?

*I pray for them.* Who has asked me to pray for them? What needs do I bring to prayer today?

# Closing Prayer

*After a period of silent reflection and/or discussion, all recite the Lord's Prayer and the following:*

The LORD is my light and my salvation;
    whom should I fear?
The LORD is my life's refuge;
    of whom should I be afraid?

One thing I ask of the LORD;
    this I seek:
To dwell in the house of the LORD
    all the days of my life,
That I may gaze on the loveliness of the LORD
    and contemplate his temple.

Hear, O Lord, the sound of my call;
    have pity on me, and answer me.
Of you my heart speaks; you my glance seeks.

*From Psalm 27*

# Living the Word This Week

*How can I make my life a gift for others in charity?*

Write a message of encouragement to someone in authority.

# MAY 31, 2020

*Lectio Divina* for the Solemnity of Pentecost

*We begin our prayer:*
In the name of the Father, and of the Son, and of the Holy Spirit. Amen.

Grant, we pray, almighty God,
that the splendor of your glory
may shine forth upon us
and that, by the bright rays of the Holy Spirit,
the light of your light may confirm the hearts
of those born again by your grace.
Through our Lord Jesus Christ, your Son,
who lives and reigns with you in the unity of the Holy Spirit,
one God, for ever and ever.

*Collect, Pentecost, Simple Vigil*

# Reading (*Lectio*)

*Read the following Scripture two or three times.*

John 20:19-23

On the evening of that first day of the week, when the doors were locked, where the disciples were, for fear of the Jews, Jesus came and stood in their midst and said to them, "Peace be with you." When he had said this, he showed them his hands and his side. The disciples rejoiced when they saw the Lord. Jesus said to them again, "Peace be with you. As the Father has sent me, so I send you." And when he had said this, he breathed on them and said to them, "Receive the Holy Spirit. Whose sins you forgive are forgiven them, and whose sins you retain are retained."

# Meditation (*Meditatio*)

*After the reading, take some time to reflect in silence on one or more of the following questions:*

- What word or words in this passage caught your attention?
- What in this passage comforted you?
- What in this passage challenged you?

*If practicing* lectio divina *as a family or in a group, after the reflection time, invite the participants to share their responses.*

# Prayer (*Oratio*)

*Read the Scripture passage one more time. Bring to the Lord the praise, petition, or thanksgiving that the Word inspires in you.*

# Contemplation (*Contemplatio*)

*Read the Scripture again, followed by this reflection:*

 What conversion of mind, heart, and life is the Lord asking of me?

*Peace be with you.* How have I experienced Christ's peace? How can I share this peace with my family, my co-workers, with the world?

*As the Father has sent me, so I send you.* How did I discern/am I discerning my vocation? How can I support others in their discernment?

*Receive the Holy Spirit.* What gifts have I received from the Holy Spirit? How can I place these gifts at the service of the community?

# Closing Prayer

*After a period of silent reflection and/or discussion, all recite the Lord's Prayer and the following:*

Come, Holy Spirit, come!
And from your celestial home
    Shed a ray of light divine!
Come, Father of the poor!
Come, source of all our store!
    Come, within our bosoms shine.
You, of comforters the best;
You, the soul's most welcome guest;
    Sweet refreshment here below;
In our labor, rest most sweet;
Grateful coolness in the heat;
    Solace in the midst of woe.
O most blessed Light divine,
Shine within these hearts of yours,
    And our inmost being fill!
Where you are not, we have naught,
Nothing good in deed or thought,
    Nothing free from taint of ill.
Heal our wounds, our strength renew;
On our dryness pour your dew;
    Wash the stains of guilt away:
Bend the stubborn heart and will;
Melt the frozen, warm the chill;
    Guide the steps that go astray.
On the faithful, who adore
And confess you, evermore
    In your sevenfold gift descend;
Give them virtue's sure reward;
Give them your salvation, Lord;

Give them joys that never end.  Amen.
Alleluia.

*Sequence for Pentecost*

# Living the Word This Week

*How can I make my life a gift for others in charity?*

Become involved in parish or diocesan evangelization efforts.

# JUNE 7, 2020

*Lectio Divina* for the Solemnity of the Most Holy Trinity

*We begin our prayer:*
In the name of the Father, and of the Son, and of the Holy
Spirit. Amen.

God our Father, who by sending into the world
the Word of truth and the Spirit of sanctification
made known to the human race your wondrous mystery,
grant us, we pray, that in professing the true faith,
we may acknowledge the Trinity of eternal glory
and adore your Unity, powerful in majesty.
Through our Lord Jesus Christ, your Son,
who lives and reigns with you in the unity of the Holy Spirit,
one God, for ever and ever.

*Collect, Solemnity of the Most Holy Trinity*

# Reading (*Lectio*)

*Read the following Scripture two or three times.*

John 3:16-18

God so loved the world that he gave his only Son,
so that everyone who believes in him might not
perish but might have eternal life. For God did not
send his Son into the world to condemn the world, but
that the world might be saved through him. Whoever
believes in him will not be condemned, but whoever

does not believe has already been condemned, because
he has not believed in the name of the only Son
of God.

# Meditation (*Meditatio*)

*After the reading, take some time to reflect in silence on one or more
of the following questions:*

- What word or words in this passage caught
  your attention?
- What in this passage comforted you?
- What in this passage challenged you?

*If practicing* lectio divina *as a family or in a group, after the
reflection time, invite the participants to share their responses.*

# Prayer (*Oratio*)

*Read the Scripture passage one more time. Bring to the Lord the
praise, petition, or thanksgiving that the Word inspires in you.*

# Contemplation (*Contemplatio*)

*Read the Scripture again, followed by this reflection:*

 What conversion of mind, heart, and life is the
Lord asking of me?

*God so loved the world that he gave his only Son.* How can I share God's love with the world? How I am willing to give of myself in love?

 *For God did not send his Son into the world to condemn the world, but that the world might be saved through him.* Whom have I judged too harshly? How can I engage the broader culture in faith?

 *Whoever believes in him will not be condemned.* Do I know anyone who is searching for God? How can I accompany them on their journey?

# Closing Prayer

*After a period of silent reflection and/or discussion, all recite the Lord's Prayer and the following:*

Blessed are you, O Lord, the God of our fathers,
    praiseworthy and exalted above all forever;
And blessed is your holy and glorious name,
    praiseworthy and exalted above all for all ages.

Blessed are you in the temple of your holy glory,
    praiseworthy and glorious above all forever.

Blessed are you on the throne of your kingdom,
    praiseworthy and exalted above all forever.

Blessed are you who look into the depths
    from your throne upon the cherubim,
    praiseworthy and exalted above all forever.

*From Daniel 3*

# Living the Word This Week

*How can I make my life a gift for others in charity?*

Every day this week, pray for some event or need that you see in the headlines.

# JUNE 14, 2020

*Lectio Divina* for the Solemnity of the Most Holy Body and Blood of Christ (Corpus Christi)

*We begin our prayer:*
In the name of the Father, and of the Son, and of the Holy Spirit. Amen.

O God, who in this wonderful Sacrament
have left us a memorial of your Passion,
grant us, we pray,
so to revere the sacred mysteries of your Body and Blood
that we may always experience in ourselves
the fruits of your redemption.
Who live and reign with God the Father
in the unity of the Holy Spirit,
one God, for ever and ever.

*Collect, Solemnity of the Most Holy Body and Blood of Christ*

# Reading (*Lectio*)

*Read the following Scripture two or three times.*

John 6:51-58

Jesus said to the Jewish crowds: "I am the living bread that came down from heaven; whoever eats this bread will live forever; and the bread that I will give is my flesh for the life of the world."

The Jews quarreled among themselves, saying, "How can this man give us his flesh to eat?" Jesus said to them, "Amen, amen, I say to you, unless you eat the flesh of the Son of Man and drink his blood, you do not have life within you. Whoever eats my flesh and drinks my blood has eternal life, and I will raise him on the last day. For my flesh is true food, and my blood is true drink. Whoever eats my flesh and drinks my blood remains in me and I in him. Just as the living Father sent me and I have life because of the Father, so also the one who feeds on me will have life because of me. This is the bread that came down from heaven. Unlike your ancestors who ate and still died, whoever eats this bread will live forever."

# Meditation (*Meditatio*)

*After the reading, take some time to reflect in silence on one or more of the following questions:*

- What word or words in this passage caught your attention?
- What in this passage comforted you?
- What in this passage challenged you?

*If practicing* lectio divina *as a family or in a group, after the reflection time, invite the participants to share their responses.*

# Prayer (*Oratio*)

*Read the Scripture passage one more time. Bring to the Lord the praise, petition, or thanksgiving that the Word inspires in you.*

# Contemplation (*Contemplatio*)

*Read the Scripture again, followed by this reflection:*

 What conversion of mind, heart, and life is the Lord asking of me?

 *The bread that I will give is my flesh for the life of the world.* How can I give of myself more freely and more generously? How can I be more responsive to the needs of those who live far from me?

 *Unless you eat the flesh of the Son of Man and drink his blood, you do not have life within you.* What religious practices strengthen my faith? What religious practices strengthen my resolve to follow God's will for me?

*Whoever eats my flesh and drinks my blood remains in me and I in him.* When do I feel closest to God? When do I feel most distant?

# Closing Prayer

*After a period of silent reflection and/or discussion, all recite the Lord's Prayer and the following:*

Glorify the LORD, O Jerusalem;
    praise your God, O Zion.
For he has strengthened the bars of your gates;
    he has blessed your children within you.

He has granted peace in your borders;
    with the best of wheat he fills you.
He sends forth his command to the earth;
    swiftly runs his word!

He has proclaimed his word to Jacob,
    his statutes and his ordinances to Israel.
He has not done thus for any other nation;
    his ordinances he has not made known to them. Alleluia.

*From Psalm 147*

# Living the Word This Week

*How can I make my life a gift for others in charity?*

Spend an hour in prayer before the Blessed Sacrament.

# June 19, 2020

*Lectio Divina* for the Solemnity of the Most Sacred Heart of Jesus

*We begin our prayer:*
In the name of the Father, and of the Son, and of the Holy Spirit. Amen.

Grant, we pray, almighty God,
that we, who glory in the Heart of your beloved Son
and recall the wonders of his love for us,
may be made worthy to receive
an overflowing measure of grace
from that fount of heavenly gifts.
Through our Lord Jesus Christ, your Son,
who lives and reigns with you in the unity of the Holy Spirit,
one God, for ever and ever.

*Collect, Solemnity of the Most Sacred Heart*

# Reading (*Lectio*)

*Read the following Scripture two or three times.*

Matthew 11:25-30

At that time Jesus exclaimed: "I give praise to you, Father, Lord of heaven and earth, for although you have hidden these things from the wise and the learned you have revealed them to little ones. Yes, Father, such has been your gracious will. All things have been handed over to me by my Father. No one knows the Son except the Father, and no one knows the Father except the Son and anyone to whom the Son wishes to reveal him.

"Come to me, all you who labor and are burdened, and I will give you rest. Take my yoke upon you and learn from me, for I am meek and humble of heart; and you will find rest for yourselves. For my yoke is easy, and my burden light."

# Meditation (*Meditatio*)

*After the reading, take some time to reflect in silence on one or more of the following questions:*

- What word or words in this passage caught your attention?
- What in this passage comforted you?
- What in this passage challenged you?

*If practicing* lectio divina *as a family or in a group, after the reflection time, invite the participants to share their responses.*

# Prayer (*Oratio*)

*Read the Scripture passage one more time. Bring to the Lord the praise, petition, or thanksgiving that the Word inspires in you.*

# Contemplation (*Contemplatio*)

*Read the Scripture again, followed by this reflection:*

 What conversion of mind, heart, and life is the Lord asking of me?

 *Although you have hidden these things from the wise and the learned you have revealed them to little ones.* What areas of my faith do I need to study more? How docile am I to the teaching of the Church?

 *No one knows the Son except the Father, and no one knows the Father except the Son and anyone to whom the Son wishes to reveal him.* What efforts do I make to grow in my knowledge of and love for God? How can I show Christ's love to those I meet?

*For my yoke is easy, and my burden light.* With what burdens am I struggling? How can I help others bear their burdens?

# Closing Prayer

*After a period of silent reflection and/or discussion, all recite the Lord's Prayer and the following:*

Bless the LORD, O my soul;
    all my being, bless his holy name.
Bless the LORD, O my soul;
    and forget not all his benefits.

He pardons all your iniquities,
    heals all your ills.
He redeems your life from destruction,
    crowns you with kindness and compassion.

Merciful and gracious is the LORD,
    slow to anger and abounding in kindness.
Not according to our sins does he deal with us,
    nor does he requite us according to our crimes.

*From Psalm 103*

# Living the Word This Week

*How can I make my life a gift for others in charity?*

Consider volunteering as a catechist for children or adults.

# June 21, 2020

*Lectio Divina* for the Twelfth Week in Ordinary Time

*We begin our prayer:*
In the name of the Father, and of the Son, and of the Holy Spirit. Amen.

Grant, O Lord,
that we may always revere and love your holy name,
for you never deprive of your guidance
those you set firm on the foundation of your love.
Through our Lord Jesus Christ, your Son,
who lives and reigns with you in the unity of the Holy Spirit,
one God, for ever and ever.

*Collect, Twelfth Sunday in Ordinary Time*

# Reading (*Lectio*)

*Read the following Scripture two or three times.*

Matthew 10:26-33

Jesus said to the Twelve: "Fear no one. Nothing is concealed that will not be revealed, nor secret that will not be known. What I say to you in the darkness, speak in the light; what you hear whispered, proclaim on the housetops. And do not be afraid of those who kill the body but cannot kill the soul; rather, be afraid of the one who can destroy both soul and body in Gehenna. Are not two sparrows sold for a small coin? Yet not one of them falls to the ground without your

Father's knowledge. Even all the hairs of your head are counted. So do not be afraid; you are worth more than many sparrows. Everyone who acknowledges me before others I will acknowledge before my heavenly Father. But whoever denies me before others, I will deny before my heavenly Father."

# Meditation (*Meditatio*)

*After the reading, take some time to reflect in silence on one or more of the following questions:*

- What word or words in this passage caught your attention?
- What in this passage comforted you?
- What in this passage challenged you?

*If practicing* lectio divina *as a family or in a group, after the reflection time, invite the participants to share their responses.*

# Prayer (*Oratio*)

*Read the Scripture passage one more time. Bring to the Lord the praise, petition, or thanksgiving that the Word inspires in you.*

# Contemplation (*Contemplatio*)

*Read the Scripture again, followed by this reflection:*

 What conversion of mind, heart, and life is the Lord asking of me?

*Nothing is concealed that will not be revealed, nor secret that will not be known.* How and why do I hide my true self from others? What secret parts of my life do I need to bring to God for healing?

*What I say to you in the darkness, speak in the light.* How have I shared my faith in recent weeks? How does my way of living reflect what I believe?

*So do not be afraid; you are worth more than many sparrows.* How do my interactions with others in person and on social media reflect their dignity and worth? What people or groups in my community are not treated as valued children of God?

# Closing Prayer

*After a period of silent reflection and/or discussion, all recite the Lord's Prayer and the following:*

> For your sake I bear insult,
>> and shame covers my face.
> I have become an outcast to my brothers,
>> a stranger to my children,
> Because zeal for your house consumes me,
>> and the insults of those who blaspheme you fall
>>> upon me.
>
> I pray to you, O Lord,
>> for the time of your favor, O God!
> In your great kindness answer me
>> with your constant help.
> Answer me, O Lord, for bounteous is your kindness;
>> in your great mercy turn toward me.
>
> "See, you lowly ones, and be glad;
>> you who seek God, may your hearts revive!
> For the Lord hears the poor,
>> and his own who are in bonds he spurns not.
> Let the heavens and the earth praise him,
>> the seas and whatever moves in them!"

*From Psalm 69*

# Living the Word This Week

*How can I make my life a gift for others in charity?*

Share your faith by taking some action that supports the dignity of all human beings: write to a legislator, feed the homeless, support women in crisis pregnancies, etc.

# June 28, 2020

*Lectio Divina* for the Thirteenth Week in Ordinary Time

*We begin our prayer:*

In the name of the Father, and of the Son, and of the Holy Spirit. Amen.

O God, who through the grace of adoption
chose us to be children of light,
grant, we pray,
that we may not be wrapped in the darkness of error
but always be seen to stand in the bright light of truth.
Through our Lord Jesus Christ, your Son,
who lives and reigns with you in the unity of the Holy Spirit,
one God, for ever and ever.

*Collect, Thirteenth Sunday in Ordinary Time*

# Reading (*Lectio*)

*Read the following Scripture two or three times.*

Matthew 10:37-42

Jesus said to his apostles: "Whoever loves father or mother more than me is not worthy of me, and whoever loves son or daughter more than me is not worthy of me; and whoever does not take up his cross and follow after me is not worthy of me. Whoever finds his life will lose it, and whoever loses his life for my sake will find it.

"Whoever receives you receives me, and whoever receives me receives the one who sent me. Whoever receives a prophet because he is a prophet will receive a prophet's reward, and whoever receives a righteous man because he is a righteous man will receive a righteous man's reward. And whoever gives only a cup of cold water to one of these little ones to drink because the little one is a disciple—amen, I say to you, he will surely not lose his reward."

# Meditation (*Meditatio*)

*After the reading, take some time to reflect in silence on one or more of the following questions:*

- What word or words in this passage caught your attention?
- What in this passage comforted you?
- What in this passage challenged you?

*If practicing* lectio divina *as a family or in a group, after the reflection time, invite the participants to share their responses.*

# Prayer (*Oratio*)

*Read the Scripture passage one more time. Bring to the Lord the praise, petition, or thanksgiving that the Word inspires in you.*

# Contemplation (*Contemplatio*)

*Read the Scripture again, followed by this reflection:*

 What conversion of mind, heart, and life is the Lord asking of me?

 *Whoever does not take up his cross and follow after me is not worthy of me.* What cross is Jesus asking me to carry this week? Is there someone I can help to carry his or her cross?

 *Whoever finds his life will lose it, and whoever loses his life for my sake will find it.* What people and experiences do I find life-giving? How can I lay down my life to serve God and others?

*Whoever receives you receives me, and whoever receives me receives the one who sent me.* When has Jesus come to me in disguise? How can I be more attentive to opportunities to encounter Christ?

# Closing Prayer

*After a period of silent reflection and/or discussion, all recite the Lord's Prayer and the following:*

The promises of the LORD I will sing forever,
    through all generations my mouth shall proclaim your
        faithfulness.
For you have said, "My kindness is established forever;"
    in heaven you have confirmed your faithfulness.

Blessed the people who know the joyful shout;
    in the light of your countenance, O LORD, they walk.
At your name they rejoice all the day,
    and through your justice they are exalted.

You are the splendor of their strength,
    and by your favor our horn is exalted.
For to the LORD belongs our shield,
    and the Holy One of Israel, our king.

*From Psalm 89*

# Living the Word This Week

*How can I make my life a gift for others in charity?*

Volunteer for a parish ministry that performs corporal works of mercy.

# July 5, 2020

*We begin our prayer:*
In the name of the Father, and of the Son, and of the Holy
Spirit. Amen.

O God, who in the abasement of your Son
have raised up a fallen world,
fill your faithful with holy joy,
for on those you have rescued from slavery to sin
you bestow eternal gladness.
Through our Lord Jesus Christ, your Son,
who lives and reigns with you in the unity of the Holy Spirit,
one God, for ever and ever.

*Collect, Fourteenth Sunday in Ordinary Time*

# Reading (*Lectio*)

*Read the following Scripture two or three times.*

Matthew 11:25-30

At that time Jesus exclaimed: "I give praise to you,
Father, Lord of heaven and earth, for although
you have hidden these things from the wise and the
learned you have revealed them to little ones. Yes,
Father, such has been your gracious will. All things
have been handed over to me by my Father. No one
knows the Son except the Father, and no one knows

the Father except the Son and anyone to whom the Son wishes to reveal him.

"Come to me, all you who labor and are burdened, and I will give you rest. Take my yoke upon you and learn from me, for I am meek and humble of heart; and you will find rest for yourselves. For my yoke is easy, and my burden light."

# Meditation (*Meditatio*)

*After the reading, take some time to reflect in silence on one or more of the following questions:*

- What word or words in this passage caught your attention?
- What in this passage comforted you?
- What in this passage challenged you?

*If practicing* lectio divina *as a family or in a group, after the reflection time, invite the participants to share their responses.*

# Prayer (*Oratio*)

*Read the Scripture passage one more time. Bring to the Lord the praise, petition, or thanksgiving that the Word inspires in you.*

# Contemplation (*Contemplatio*)

*Read the Scripture again, followed by this reflection:*

 What conversion of mind, heart, and life is the Lord asking of me?

 *Although you have hidden these things from the wise and the learned you have revealed them to little ones.* How can I grow in humility? How can I be a lifelong learner about my faith?

 *No one knows the Son except the Father, and no one knows the Father except the Son and anyone to whom the Son wishes to reveal him.* How do I come to know God better? How can I help others know God?

*For my yoke is easy, and my burden light.* What burdens do I need to turn over to the Lord? When have I felt God supporting me in a difficult time?

# Closing Prayer

*After a period of silent reflection and/or discussion, all recite the Lord's Prayer and the following:*

I will extol you, O my God and King,
    and I will bless your name forever and ever.
Every day will I bless you,
    and I will praise your name forever and ever.

The LORD is gracious and merciful,
    slow to anger and of great kindness.
The LORD is good to all
    and compassionate toward all his works.

Let all your works give you thanks, O LORD,
    and let your faithful ones bless you.
Let them discourse of the glory of your kingdom
    and speak of your might.

The LORD is faithful in all his words
    and holy in all his works.

The Lord lifts up all who are falling
  and raises up all who are bowed down.

*From Psalm 145*

# Living the Word This Week

*How can I make my life a gift for others in charity?*

Read the bishops' pastoral statement on evangelization, *Go and Make Disciples: www.usccb.org/beliefs-and-teachings/how-we-teach/evangelization/go-and-make-disciples/go-and-make-disciples-a-national-plan-and-strategy-for-catholic-evangelization-in-the-united-states.cfm.*

# July 12, 2020

*Lectio Divina* for the Fifteenth Week in Ordinary Time

*We begin our prayer:*
In the name of the Father, and of the Son, and of the Holy
Spirit. Amen.

O God, who show the light of your truth
to those who go astray,
so that they may return to the right path,
give all who for the faith they profess
are accounted Christians
the grace to reject whatever is contrary to the name of Christ
and to strive after all that does it honor.
Through our Lord Jesus Christ, your Son,
who lives and reigns with you in the unity of the Holy Spirit,
one God, for ever and ever.

*Collect, Fifteenth Sunday in Ordinary Time*

# Reading (*Lectio*)

*Read the following Scripture two or three times.*

Matthew 13:1-23

On that day, Jesus went out of the house and sat
down by the sea. Such large crowds gathered
around him that he got into a boat and sat down, and
the whole crowd stood along the shore.

And he spoke to them at length in parables, saying: "A sower went out to sow. And as he sowed, some seed fell on the path, and birds came and ate it up. Some fell on rocky ground, where it had little soil. It sprang up at once because the soil was not deep, and when the sun rose it was scorched, and it withered for lack of roots. Some seed fell among thorns, and the thorns grew up and choked it. But some seed fell on rich soil, and produced fruit, a hundred or sixty or thirtyfold. Whoever has ears ought to hear."

The disciples approached him and said, "Why do you speak to them in parables?" He said to them in reply, "Because knowledge of the mysteries of the kingdom of heaven has been granted to you, but to them it has not been granted. To anyone who has, more will be given and he will grow rich; from anyone who has not, even what he has will be taken away. This is why I speak to them in parables, because *they look but do not see and hear but do not listen or understand.* Isaiah's prophecy is fulfilled in them, which says:

*You shall indeed hear but not understand,*
    *you shall indeed look but never see.*
*Gross is the heart of this people,*
    *they will hardly hear with their ears,*
    *they have closed their eyes,*
    *lest they see with their eyes*
    *and hear with their ears*
*and understand with their hearts and be converted,*
    *and I heal them.*

"But blessed are your eyes, because they see, and your ears, because they hear. Amen, I say to you, many prophets and righteous people longed to see what you see but did not see it, and to hear what you hear but did not hear it.

"Hear then the parable of the sower. The seed sown on the path is the one who hears the word of the kingdom without understanding it, and the evil one comes and steals away what was sown in his heart. The seed sown on rocky ground is the one who hears the word and receives it at once with joy. But he has no root and lasts only for a time. When some tribulation or persecution comes because of the word, he immediately falls away. The seed sown among thorns is the one who hears the word, but then worldly anxiety and the lure of riches choke the word and it bears no fruit. But the seed sown on rich soil is the one who hears the word and understands it, who indeed bears fruit and yields a hundred or sixty or thirtyfold."

# Meditation (*Meditatio*)

*After the reading, take some time to reflect in silence on one or more of the following questions:*

- What word or words in this passage caught your attention?
- What in this passage comforted you?
- What in this passage challenged you?

*If practicing* lectio divina *as a family or in a group, after the reflection time, invite the participants to share their responses.*

# Prayer (*Oratio*)

*Read the Scripture passage one more time. Bring to the Lord the praise, petition, or thanksgiving that the Word inspires in you.*

# Contemplation (*Contemplatio*)

*Read the Scripture again, followed by this reflection:*

 What conversion of mind, heart, and life is the Lord asking of me?

 *They look but do not see and hear but do not listen or understand.* What keeps me from paying attention to God's presence and action in my life? When do I fail to listen and try to understand others?

*Worldly anxiety and the lure of riches choke the word and it bears no fruit.* What anxieties keep me from doing God's will? What temptations lure me away from God's path?

 *But the seed sown on rich soil is the one who hears the word and understands it, who indeed bears fruit.* How does my faith bear fruit in my life? How can I make my heart rich soil for God's word?

# Closing Prayer

*After a period of silent reflection and/or discussion, all recite the Lord's Prayer and the following:*

You have visited the land and watered it;
    greatly have you enriched it.
God's watercourses are filled;
    you have prepared the grain.

Thus have you prepared the land: drenching its furrows,
    breaking up its clods,

Softening it with showers,
  blessing its yield.

You have crowned the year with your bounty,
  and your paths overflow with a rich harvest;
The untilled meadows overflow with it,
  and rejoicing clothes the hills.

The fields are garmented with flocks
  and the valleys blanketed with grain.
  They shout and sing for joy.

*From Psalm 65*

# Living the Word This Week

*How can I make my life a gift for others in charity?*

Spend time each day this week praying the Mass readings.

# July 19, 2020

*Lectio Divina* for the Sixteenth Week in Ordinary Time

*We begin our prayer:*
In the name of the Father, and of the Son, and of the Holy Spirit. Amen.

Show favor, O Lord, to your servants
and mercifully increase the gifts of your grace,
that, made fervent in hope, faith and charity,
they may be ever watchful in keeping your commands.
Through our Lord Jesus Christ, your Son,
who lives and reigns with you in the unity of the Holy Spirit,
one God, for ever and ever.

*Collect, Sixteenth Sunday in Ordinary Time*

# Reading (*Lectio*)

*Read the following Scripture two or three times.*

Matthew 13:24-43

Jesus proposed another parable to the crowds, saying: "The kingdom of heaven may be likened to a man who sowed good seed in his field. While everyone was asleep his enemy came and sowed weeds all through the wheat, and then went off. When the crop grew and bore fruit, the weeds appeared as well. The slaves of the householder came to him and said, 'Master, did you not sow good seed in your field?

Where have the weeds come from?' He answered, 'An enemy has done this.' His slaves said to him, 'Do you want us to go and pull them up?' He replied, 'No, if you pull up the weeds you might uproot the wheat along with them. Let them grow together until harvest; then at harvest time I will say to the harvesters, "First collect the weeds and tie them in bundles for burning; but gather the wheat into my barn."'"

He proposed another parable to them. "The kingdom of heaven is like a mustard seed that a person took and sowed in a field. It is the smallest of all the seeds, yet when full-grown it is the largest of plants. It becomes a large bush, and the 'birds of the sky come and dwell in its branches.'"

He spoke to them another parable. "The kingdom of heaven is like yeast that a woman took and mixed with three measures of wheat flour until the whole batch was leavened."

All these things Jesus spoke to the crowds in parables. He spoke to them only in parables, to fulfill what had been said through the prophet:

*I will open my mouth in parables,*
*I will announce what has lain hidden from the*
*foundation of the world.*

Then, dismissing the crowds, he went into the house. His disciples approached him and said, "Explain to us the parable of the weeds in the field." He said in reply, "He who sows good seed is the Son of Man, the field is the world, the good seed the children of the kingdom. The weeds are the children of the evil one, and the enemy who sows them is the devil. The harvest is the end of the age, and the harvesters are angels. Just as weeds are collected and burned up with fire, so will it be at the end of the age. The Son of Man will send his angels, and they will collect out of his kingdom all who cause others to sin and all evildoers. They will throw them into the fiery furnace, where there will be wailing and grinding of teeth. Then the righteous will shine like the sun in the kingdom of their Father. Whoever has ears ought to hear."

## Meditation (*Meditatio*)

*After the reading, take some time to reflect in silence on one or more of the following questions:*

- What word or words in this passage caught your attention?
- What in this passage comforted you?
- What in this passage challenged you?

*If practicing* lectio divina *as a family or in a group, after the reflection time, invite the participants to share their responses.*

## Prayer (*Oratio*)

*Read the Scripture passage one more time. Bring to the Lord the praise, petition, or thanksgiving that the Word inspires in you.*

# Contemplation (*Contemplatio*)

*Read the Scripture again, followed by this reflection:*

 What conversion of mind, heart, and life is the Lord asking of me?

 *It is the smallest of all the seeds, yet when full-grown it is the largest of plants.* What people and opportunities help me to grow in faith? How can I nurture the seeds of faith in others?

 *The kingdom of heaven is like yeast that a woman took and mixed with three measures of wheat flour until the whole batch was leavened.* What prayers help my heart rise to God? How do I combine my faith with the rest of my daily life?

*The weeds are the children of the evil one, and the enemy who sows them is the devil. What sinful behaviors do I need to weed out of my life? What things keep me from doing God's will?*

# Closing Prayer

*After a period of silent reflection and/or discussion, all recite the Lord's Prayer and the following:*

You, O Lord, are good and forgiving,
   abounding in kindness to all who call upon you.
Hearken, O Lord, to my prayer
   and attend to the sound of my pleading.

All the nations you have made shall come
   and worship you, O Lord,
   and glorify your name.
For you are great, and you do wondrous deeds;
   you alone are God.

You, O Lord, are a God merciful and gracious,
   slow to anger, abounding in kindness and fidelity.
Turn toward me, and have pity on me;
   give your strength to your servant.

*From Psalm 86*

198

# Living the Word This Week

*How can I make my life a gift for others in charity?*

Look into your parish and diocesan offerings for adult faith formation and prayerfully consider participating.

# July 26, 2020

*Lectio Divina* for the Seventeenth Week in Ordinary Time

*We begin our prayer:*
In the name of the Father, and of the Son, and of the Holy
Spirit. Amen.

O God, protector of those who hope in you,
without whom nothing has firm foundation, nothing is holy,
bestow in abundance your mercy upon us
and grant that, with you as our ruler and guide,
we may use the good things that pass
in such a way as to hold fast even now
to those that ever endure.
Through our Lord Jesus Christ, your Son,
who lives and reigns with you in the unity of the Holy Spirit,
one God, for ever and ever.

*Collect, Seventeenth Sunday in Ordinary Time*

# Reading (*Lectio*)

*Read the following Scripture two or three times.*

Matthew 13:44-52

Jesus said to his disciples: "The kingdom of heaven
is like a treasure buried in a field, which a person
finds and hides again, and out of joy goes and sells all
that he has and buys that field. Again, the kingdom
of heaven is like a merchant searching for fine pearls.

When he finds a pearl of great price, he goes and sells all that he has and buys it. Again, the kingdom of heaven is like a net thrown into the sea, which collects fish of every kind. When it is full they haul it ashore and sit down to put what is good into buckets. What is bad they throw away. Thus it will be at the end of the age. The angels will go out and separate the wicked from the righteous and throw them into the fiery furnace, where there will be wailing and grinding of teeth.

"Do you understand all these things?" They answered, "Yes." And he replied, "Then every scribe who has been instructed in the kingdom of heaven is like the head of a household who brings from his storeroom both the new and the old."

# Meditation (*Meditatio*)

*After the reading, take some time to reflect in silence on one or more of the following questions:*

- What word or words in this passage caught your attention?
- What in this passage comforted you?
- What in this passage challenged you?

*If practicing* lectio divina *as a family or in a group, after the reflection time, invite the participants to share their responses.*

# Prayer (*Oratio*)

*Read the Scripture passage one more time. Bring to the Lord the praise, petition, or thanksgiving that the Word inspires in you.*

# Contemplation (*Contemplatio*)

*Read the Scripture again, followed by this reflection:*

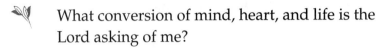 What conversion of mind, heart, and life is the Lord asking of me?

*The kingdom of heaven is like a treasure buried in a field.* What do I treasure most about my faith? When have I buried my faith?

*When he finds a pearl of great price, he goes and sells all that he has and buys it.* What have I had to sacrifice for my faith? How can I become a better steward of God's gifts?

*Every scribe who has been instructed in the kingdom of heaven is like the head of a household who brings from his storeroom both the new and the old.* What faith traditions are most meaningful to me? What steps can I take to stay abreast of what is happening in the Church?

# Closing Prayer

*After a period of silent reflection and/or discussion, all recite the Lord's Prayer and the following:*

I have said, O LORD, that my part
    is to keep your words.
The law of your mouth is to me more precious
    than thousands of gold and silver pieces.

Let your kindness comfort me
    according to your promise to your servants.
Let your compassion come to me that I may live,
    for your law is my delight.

For I love your command
    more than gold, however fine.
For in all your precepts I go forward;
    every false way I hate.

Wonderful are your decrees;
   therefore I observe them.
The revelation of your words sheds light,
   giving understanding to the simple.

*From Psalm 119*

## Living the Word This Week

*How can I make my life a gift for others in charity?*

Follow your parish, your bishop, the USCCB, and the Holy Father on social media.

# AUGUST 2, 2020

*Lectio Divina* for the Eighteenth Week in Ordinary Time

*We begin our prayer:*
In the name of the Father, and of the Son, and of the Holy
Spirit. Amen.

Draw near to your servants, O Lord,
and answer their prayers with unceasing kindness,
that, for those who glory in you as their Creator and guide,
you may restore what you have created
and keep safe what you have restored.
Through our Lord Jesus Christ, your Son,
who lives and reigns with you in the unity of the Holy Spirit,
one God, for ever and ever.

*Collect, Eighteenth Sunday in Ordinary Time*

# Reading (*Lectio*)

*Read the following Scripture two or three times.*

Matthew 14:13-21

When Jesus heard of the death of John the Baptist,
he withdrew in a boat to a deserted place by
himself. The crowds heard of this and followed him
on foot from their towns. When he disembarked
and saw the vast crowd, his heart was moved with
pity for them, and he cured their sick. When it was
evening, the disciples approached him and said, "This

is a deserted place and it is already late; dismiss the crowds so that they can go to the villages and buy food for themselves." Jesus said to them, "There is no need for them to go away; give them some food yourselves." But they said to him, "Five loaves and two fish are all we have here." Then he said, "Bring them here to me," and he ordered the crowds to sit down on the grass. Taking the five loaves and the two fish, and looking up to heaven, he said the blessing, broke the loaves, and gave them to the disciples, who in turn gave them to the crowds. They all ate and were satisfied, and they picked up the fragments left over— twelve wicker baskets full. Those who ate were about five thousand men, not counting women and children.

# Meditation (*Meditatio*)

*After the reading, take some time to reflect in silence on one or more of the following questions:*

- What word or words in this passage caught your attention?
- What in this passage comforted you?
- What in this passage challenged you?

*If practicing* lectio divina *as a family or in a group, after the reflection time, invite the participants to share their responses.*

# Prayer (*Oratio*)

*Read the Scripture passage one more time. Bring to the Lord the praise, petition, or thanksgiving that the Word inspires in you.*

# Contemplation (*Contemplatio*)

*Read the Scripture again, followed by this reflection:*

 What conversion of mind, heart, and life is the Lord asking of me?

 *The crowds heard of this and followed him on foot from their towns.* What encouraged me to follow Jesus? Where is God calling me to go?

 *His heart was moved with pity for them.* What pain do I need to entrust to the heart of Jesus? How can I be more compassionate toward others?

*There is no need for them to go away; give them some food yourselves.* How have I pushed people away from God because of my words or actions? How can I attend to others' needs more generously?

# Closing Prayer

*After a period of silent reflection and/or discussion, all recite the Lord's Prayer and the following:*

The LORD is gracious and merciful,
    slow to anger and of great kindness.
The LORD is good to all
    and compassionate toward all his works.

The eyes of all look hopefully to you,
    and you give them their food in due season;
you open your hand
    and satisfy the desire of every living thing.

The LORD is just in all his ways
    and holy in all his works.
The LORD is near to all who call upon him,
    to all who call upon him in truth.

*From Psalm 145*

# Living the Word This Week

*How can I make my life a gift for others in charity?*

Contribute time, food, or money to a local food pantry.

# AUGUST 6, 2020

*Lectio Divina* for the Transfiguration of the Lord

*We begin our prayer:*
In the name of the Father, and of the Son, and of the Holy Spirit. Amen.

O God, who in the glorious Transfiguration
of your Only Begotten Son
confirmed the mysteries of faith by the witness of the Fathers
and wonderfully prefigured our full adoption to sonship,
grant, we pray, to your servants,
that, listening to the voice of your beloved Son,
we may merit to become co-heirs with him.
Who lives and reigns with you in the unity of the Holy Spirit,
one God, for ever and ever.

*Collect, Feast of the Transfiguration of the Lord*

# Reading (*Lectio*)

*Read the following Scripture two or three times.*

Matthew 17:1-9

Jesus took Peter, James, and his brother, John, and led them up a high mountain by themselves. And he was transfigured before them; his face shone like the sun and his clothes became white as light. And behold, Moses and Elijah appeared to them, conversing with him. Then Peter said to Jesus in reply, "Lord, it is good that we are here. If you wish, I will make three tents here, one for you, one for Moses, and one for Elijah." While he was still speaking, behold, a bright cloud cast a shadow over them, then from the cloud came a voice that said, "This is my beloved Son, with whom I am well pleased; listen to him." When the disciples heard this, they fell prostrate and were very much afraid. But Jesus came and touched them, saying, "Rise, and do not be afraid." And when the disciples raised their eyes, they saw no one else but Jesus alone.

As they were coming down from the mountain, Jesus charged them, "Do not tell the vision to anyone until the Son of Man has been raised from the dead."

# Meditation (*Meditatio*)

*After the reading, take some time to reflect in silence on one or more of the following questions:*

- What word or words in this passage caught your attention?
- What in this passage comforted you?
- What in this passage challenged you?

*If practicing* lectio divina *as a family or in a group, after the reflection time, invite the participants to share their responses.*

# Prayer (*Oratio*)

*Read the Scripture passage one more time. Bring to the Lord the praise, petition, or thanksgiving that the Word inspires in you.*

# Contemplation (*Contemplatio*)

*Read the Scripture again, followed by this reflection:*

 What conversion of mind, heart, and life is the Lord asking of me?

 *And he was transfigured before them; his face shone like the sun and his clothes became white as light.* When am I most aware of God's power and majesty? How does creation point me toward God?

 *This is my beloved Son, with whom I am well pleased; listen to him.* How can I please God in my words and actions? How do I listen to the voice of God?

*And when the disciples raised their eyes, they saw no one else but Jesus alone.* How can I keep my eyes fixed on Jesus? How can I see Jesus in everyone I meet?

# Closing Prayer

*After a period of silent reflection and/or discussion, all recite the Lord's Prayer and the following:*

The LORD is king; let the earth rejoice;
    let the many islands be glad.
Clouds and darkness are round about him,
    justice and judgment are the foundation of his throne.

The mountains melt like wax before the LORD,
    before the LORD of all the earth.
The heavens proclaim his justice,
    and all peoples see his glory.

Because you, O LORD, are the Most High over all the earth,
    exalted far above all gods.

*From Psalm 97*

# Living the Word This Week

*How can I make my life a gift for others in charity?*

Read Pope Francis's Encyclical *Laudato Si', On Care for Our Common Home*: *http://w2.vatican.va/content/francesco/ en/encyclicals/documents/papa-francesco_20150524_enciclica-laudato-si.html.*

# August 9, 2020

*Lectio Divina* for the Nineteenth Week in Ordinary Time

*We begin our prayer:*
In the name of the Father, and of the Son, and of the Holy
Spirit. Amen.

Almighty ever-living God,
whom, taught by the Holy Spirit,
we dare to call our Father,
bring, we pray, to perfection in our hearts
the spirit of adoption as your sons and daughters,
that we may merit to enter into the inheritance
which you have promised.
Through our Lord Jesus Christ, your Son,
who lives and reigns with you in the unity of the Holy Spirit,
one God, for ever and ever.

*Collect, Nineteenth Sunday in Ordinary Time*

# Reading (*Lectio*)

*Read the following Scripture two or three times.*

Matthew 14:22-33

After he had fed the people, Jesus made the
disciples get into a boat and precede him to the
other side, while he dismissed the crowds. After doing
so, he went up on the mountain by himself to pray.
When it was evening he was there alone. Meanwhile

the boat, already a few miles offshore, was being tossed about by the waves, for the wind was against it. During the fourth watch of the night, he came toward them walking on the sea. When the disciples saw him walking on the sea they were terrified. "It is a ghost," they said, and they cried out in fear. At once Jesus spoke to them, "Take courage, it is I; do not be afraid." Peter said to him in reply, "Lord, if it is you, command me to come to you on the water." He said, "Come." Peter got out of the boat and began to walk on the water toward Jesus. But when he saw how strong the wind was he became frightened; and, beginning to sink, he cried out, "Lord, save me!" Immediately Jesus stretched out his hand and caught Peter, and said to him, "O you of little faith, why did you doubt?" After they got into the boat, the wind died down. Those who were in the boat did him homage, saying, "Truly, you are the Son of God."

# Meditation (*Meditatio*)

*After the reading, take some time to reflect in silence on one or more of the following questions:*

- What word or words in this passage caught your attention?
- What in this passage comforted you?
- What in this passage challenged you?

*If practicing* lectio divina *as a family or in a group, after the reflection time, invite the participants to share their responses.*

# Prayer (*Oratio*)

*Read the Scripture passage one more time. Bring to the Lord the praise, petition, or thanksgiving that the Word inspires in you.*

# Contemplation (*Contemplatio*)

*Read the Scripture again, followed by this reflection:*

 What conversion of mind, heart, and life is the Lord asking of me?

 *Peter said to him in reply, "Lord, if it is you, command me to come to you on the water."* When have I tested the Lord's love for me? What do I need to find the courage to do?

*But when he saw how strong the wind was he became frightened; and, beginning to sink, he cried out, "Lord, save me!"* From what do I need Jesus to save me? What burdens make me feel like I might sink?

 *O you of little faith, why did you doubt?* When have I doubted God? What renewed my faith and trust?

# Closing Prayer

*After a period of silent reflection and/or discussion, all recite the Lord's Prayer and the following:*

> I will hear what God proclaims;
>     the LORD—for he proclaims peace.
> Near indeed is his salvation to those who fear him,
>     glory dwelling in our land.
>
> Kindness and truth shall meet;
>     justice and peace shall kiss.

Truth shall spring out of the earth,
   and justice shall look down from heaven.

The LORD himself will give his benefits;
   our land shall yield its increase.
Justice shall walk before him,
   and prepare the way of his steps.

*From Psalm 85*

# Living the Word This Week

*How can I make my life a gift for others in charity?*

Believing in God's saving mercy, receive the Sacrament
of Penance.

# AUGUST 16, 2020

*Lectio Divina* for the Twentieth Week in Ordinary Time

*We begin our prayer:*
In the name of the Father, and of the Son, and of the Holy Spirit. Amen.

O God, who have prepared for those who love you
good things which no eye can see,
fill our hearts, we pray, with the warmth of your love,
so that, loving you in all things and above all things,
we may attain your promises,
which surpass every human desire.
Through our Lord Jesus Christ, your Son,
who lives and reigns with you in the unity of the Holy Spirit,
one God, for ever and ever.

*Collect, Twentieth Sunday in Ordinary Time*

# Reading (*Lectio*)

*Read the following Scripture two or three times.*

Matthew 15:21-28

At that time, Jesus withdrew to the region of Tyre and Sidon. And behold, a Canaanite woman of that district came and called out, "Have pity on me, Lord, Son of David! My daughter is tormented by a demon." But Jesus did not say a word in answer to her. Jesus' disciples came and asked him, "Send her away, for she keeps calling out after us." He said in reply, "I was sent only to the lost sheep of the house of Israel." But the woman came and did Jesus homage, saying, "Lord, help me." He said in reply, "It is not right to take the food of the children and throw it to the dogs." She said, "Please, Lord, for even the dogs eat the scraps that fall from the table of their masters." Then Jesus said to her in reply, "O woman, great is your faith! Let it be done for you as you wish." And the woman's daughter was healed from that hour.

# Meditation (*Meditatio*)

*After the reading, take some time to reflect in silence on one or more of the following questions:*

- What word or words in this passage caught your attention?
- What in this passage comforted you?
- What in this passage challenged you?

*If practicing* lectio divina *as a family or in a group, after the reflection time, invite the participants to share their responses.*

# Prayer (*Oratio*)

*Read the Scripture passage one more time. Bring to the Lord the praise, petition, or thanksgiving that the Word inspires in you.*

# Contemplation (*Contemplatio*)

*Read the Scripture again, followed by this reflection:*

 What conversion of mind, heart, and life is the Lord asking of me?

 *But Jesus did not say a word in answer to her.* When has God seemed silent in my life? When have I been silent in the face of others' needs?

 *I was sent only to the lost sheep of the house of Israel.* Where is God sending me? How can I participate more fully in the Church's evangelizing mission?

*O woman, great is your faith! Let it be done for you as you wish.* When has God answered my prayers? Who has been a model of faith for me?

# Closing Prayer

*After a period of silent reflection and/or discussion, all recite the Lord's Prayer and the following:*

May God have pity on us and bless us;
  may he let his face shine upon us.
So may your way be known upon earth;
  among all nations, your salvation.

May the nations be glad and exult
  because you rule the peoples in equity;
    the nations on the earth you guide.

May the peoples praise you, O God;
  may all the peoples praise you!
May God bless us,
  and may all the ends of the earth fear him!

*From Psalm 67*

# Living the Word This Week

*How can I make my life a gift for others in charity?*

**Read** *Living as Missionary Disciples: A Resource for Evangelization: http://ccc.usccb.org/flipbooks/ living-as-missionary-disciples/.*

# AUGUST 23, 2020

*Lectio Divina* for the Twenty-First Week in Ordinary Time

*We begin our prayer:*
In the name of the Father, and of the Son, and of the Holy
Spirit. Amen.

O God, who cause the minds of the faithful
to unite in a single purpose,
grant your people to love what you command
and to desire what you promise,
that, amid the uncertainties of this world,
our hearts may be fixed on that place
where true gladness is found.
Through our Lord Jesus Christ, your Son,
who lives and reigns with you in the unity of the Holy Spirit,
one God, for ever and ever.

*Collect, Twenty-First Sunday in Ordinary Time*

# Reading (*Lectio*)

*Read the following Scripture two or three times.*

Matthew 16:13-20

Jesus went into the region of Caesarea Philippi and
he asked his disciples, "Who do people say that
the Son of Man is?" They replied, "Some say John the
Baptist, others Elijah, still others Jeremiah or one of the
prophets." He said to them, "But who do you say that

I am?" Simon Peter said in reply, "You are the Christ, the Son of the living God." Jesus said to him in reply, "Blessed are you, Simon son of Jonah. For flesh and blood has not revealed this to you, but my heavenly Father. And so I say to you, you are Peter, and upon this rock I will build my church, and the gates of the netherworld shall not prevail against it. I will give you the keys to the kingdom of heaven. Whatever you bind on earth shall be bound in heaven; and whatever you loose on earth shall be loosed in heaven." Then he strictly ordered his disciples to tell no one that he was the Christ.

# Meditation (*Meditatio*)

*After the reading, take some time to reflect in silence on one or more of the following questions:*

- What word or words in this passage caught your attention?
- What in this passage comforted you?
- What in this passage challenged you?

*If practicing* lectio divina *as a family or in a group, after the reflection time, invite the participants to share their responses.*

# Prayer (*Oratio*)

*Read the Scripture passage one more time. Bring to the Lord the praise, petition, or thanksgiving that the Word inspires in you.*

# Contemplation (*Contemplatio*)

*Read the Scripture again, followed by this reflection:*

 What conversion of mind, heart, and life is the Lord asking of me?

 *But who do you say that I am?* How would I describe Jesus? How has my image of Jesus changed throughout my life?

 *For flesh and blood has not revealed this to you, but my heavenly Father.* How have I come to know God through Scripture and Tradition? How can I continue to encounter Christ?

*Upon this rock I will build my church, and the gates of the netherworld shall not prevail against it.* How do I support my parish, my diocese, and the universal Church? What can I do to strengthen the Church?

# Closing Prayer

*After a period of silent reflection and/or discussion, all recite the Lord's Prayer and the following:*

I will give thanks to you, O Lord, with all my heart,
    for you have heard the words of my mouth;
in the presence of the angels I will sing your praise;
    I will worship at your holy temple.

I will give thanks to your name,
    because of your kindness and your truth:
When I called, you answered me;
    you built up strength within me.

The Lord is exalted, yet the lowly he sees,
    and the proud he knows from afar.
Your kindness, O Lord, endures forever;
    forsake not the work of your hands.

*From Psalm 138*

# Living the Word This Week

*How can I make my life a gift for others in charity?*

Pray for the intentions of the Holy Father: *http://www.usccb. org/prayer-and-worship/prayers-and-devotions/the-popes-monthly-intention.cfm.*

# August 30, 2020

*Lectio Divina* for the Twenty-Second Week in
Ordinary Time

*We begin our prayer:*
In the name of the Father, and of the Son, and of the Holy
Spirit. Amen.

God of might, giver of every good gift,
put into our hearts the love of your name,
so that, by deepening our sense of reverence,
you may nurture in us what is good
and, by your watchful care,
keep safe what you have nurtured.
Through our Lord Jesus Christ, your Son,
who lives and reigns with you in the unity of the Holy Spirit,
one God, for ever and ever.

*Collect, Twenty-Second Sunday in Ordinary Time*

# Reading (*Lectio*)

*Read the following Scripture two or three times.*

Matthew 16:21-27

Jesus began to show his disciples that he must go
to Jerusalem and suffer greatly from the elders, the
chief priests, and the scribes, and be killed and on the
third day be raised. Then Peter took Jesus aside and
began to rebuke him, "God forbid, Lord! No such

thing shall ever happen to you." He turned and said to Peter, "Get behind me, Satan! You are an obstacle to me. You are thinking not as God does, but as human beings do."

Then Jesus said to his disciples, "Whoever wishes to come after me must deny himself, take up his cross, and follow me. For whoever wishes to save his life will lose it, but whoever loses his life for my sake will find it. What profit would there be for one to gain the whole world and forfeit his life? Or what can one give in exchange for his life? For the Son of Man will come with his angels in his Father's glory, and then he will repay all according to his conduct."

# Meditation (*Meditatio*)

*After the reading, take some time to reflect in silence on one or more of the following questions:*

- What word or words in this passage caught your attention?
- What in this passage comforted you?
- What in this passage challenged you?

*If practicing* lectio divina *as a family or in a group, after the reflection time, invite the participants to share their responses.*

# Prayer (*Oratio*)

*Read the Scripture passage one more time. Bring to the Lord the praise, petition, or thanksgiving that the Word inspires in you.*

# Contemplation (*Contemplatio*)

*Read the Scripture again, followed by this reflection:*

 What conversion of mind, heart, and life is the Lord asking of me?

 *Jesus began to show his disciples that he must go to Jerusalem and suffer greatly.* How can I grow in gratitude for Jesus' suffering and the salvation it brought? What daily difficulties or struggles can I offer to the Lord?

 *You are thinking not as God does, but as human beings do.* When do I place the world's values above God's commandments? How can I learn to discern what God wants from me?

*Whoever wishes to come after me must deny himself, take up his cross, and follow me.* What cross do I need to bear? How can I give of myself to help others bear their crosses?

# Closing Prayer

*After a period of silent reflection and/or discussion, all recite the Lord's Prayer and the following:*

O God, you are my God whom I seek;
   for you my flesh pines and my soul thirsts
like the earth, parched, lifeless and without water.

Thus have I gazed toward you in the sanctuary
   to see your power and your glory,
For your kindness is a greater good than life;
   my lips shall glorify you.

Thus will I bless you while I live;
   lifting up my hands, I will call upon your name.
As with the riches of a banquet shall my soul be satisfied,
   and with exultant lips my mouth shall praise you.

You are my help,
   and in the shadow of your wings I shout for joy.
My soul clings fast to you;
   your right hand upholds me.

*From Psalm 63*

# Living the Word This Week

*How can I make my life a gift for others in charity?*

Learn more about Christians around the world who are persecuted for their faith: *www.usccb.org/issues-and-action/ religious-liberty/international-religious-freedom.cfm.*

# September 6, 2020

*Lectio Divina* for the Twenty-Third Week in Ordinary Time

*We begin our prayer:*
In the name of the Father, and of the Son, and of the Holy Spirit. Amen.

O God, by whom we are redeemed and receive adoption,
look graciously upon your beloved sons and daughters,
that those who believe in Christ
may receive true freedom
and an everlasting inheritance.
Through our Lord Jesus Christ, your Son,
who lives and reigns with you in the unity of the Holy Spirit,
one God, for ever and ever.

*Collect, Twenty-Third Sunday in Ordinary Time*

# Reading (*Lectio*)

*Read the following Scripture two or three times.*

Matthew 18:15-20

Jesus said to his disciples: "If your brother sins against you, go and tell him his fault between you and him alone. If he listens to you, you have won over your brother. If he does not listen, take one or two others along with you, so that 'every fact may be established on the testimony of two or three witnesses.' If he refuses to listen to them, tell the church. If he refuses to listen even to the church, then treat him as you would a Gentile or a tax collector. Amen, I say to you, whatever you bind on earth shall be bound in heaven, and whatever you loose on earth shall be loosed in heaven. Again, amen, I say to you, if two of you agree on earth about anything for which they are to pray, it shall be granted to them by my heavenly Father. For where two or three are gathered together in my name, there am I in the midst of them."

# Meditation (*Meditatio*)

*After the reading, take some time to reflect in silence on one or more of the following questions:*

- What word or words in this passage caught your attention?
- What in this passage comforted you?
- What in this passage challenged you?

*If practicing* lectio divina *as a family or in a group, after the reflection time, invite the participants to share their responses.*

# Prayer (*Oratio*)

*Read the Scripture passage one more time. Bring to the Lord the praise, petition, or thanksgiving that the Word inspires in you.*

# Contemplation (*Contemplatio*)

*Read the Scripture again, followed by this reflection:*

🌱 What conversion of mind, heart, and life is the Lord asking of me?

🌱 *If your brother sins against you, go and tell him his fault between you and him alone.* How can I speak the truth in love to my family and friends? How can I offer guidance and forgiveness in love and humility?

🌱 *Whatever you bind on earth shall be bound in heaven, and whatever you loose on earth shall be loosed in heaven.* How can I grow in fidelity to Church teaching, especially those I struggle to accept? How can I submit my will to God?

*For where two or three are gathered together in my name, there am I in the midst of them.* What faith communities (small or large) am I part of? How can I find more opportunities for communal prayer?

# Closing Prayer

*After a period of silent reflection and/or discussion, all recite the Lord's Prayer and the following:*

Come, let us sing joyfully to the LORD;
    let us acclaim the rock of our salvation.
Let us come into his presence with thanksgiving;
    let us joyfully sing psalms to him.

Come, let us bow down in worship;
    let us kneel before the LORD who made us.
For he is our God,
    and we are the people he shepherds, the flock he guides.

Oh, that today you would hear his voice:
    "Harden not your hearts as at Meribah,
    as in the day of Massah in the desert,
Where your fathers tempted me;
    they tested me though they had seen my works."

*From Psalm 95*

# Living the Word This Week

*How can I make my life a gift for others in charity?*

Attend Sunday Mass and be aware of Christ present in the gathered community.

# September 13, 2020

*Lectio Divina* for the Twenty-Fourth Week in
Ordinary Time

*We begin our prayer:*
In the name of the Father, and of the Son, and of the Holy
Spirit. Amen.

Look upon us, O God,
Creator and ruler of all things,
and, that we may feel the working of your mercy,
grant that we may serve you with all our heart.
Through our Lord Jesus Christ, your Son,
who lives and reigns with you in the unity of the Holy Spirit,
one God, for ever and ever.

*Collect, Twenty-Fourth Sunday in Ordinary Time*

# Reading (*Lectio*)

*Read the following Scripture two or three times.*

Matthew 18:21-35

Peter approached Jesus and asked him, "Lord, if my
brother sins against me, how often must I forgive?
As many as seven times?" Jesus answered, "I say to
you, not seven times but seventy-seven times. That
is why the kingdom of heaven may be likened to a
king who decided to settle accounts with his servants.
When he began the accounting, a debtor was brought

before him who owed him a huge amount. Since he had no way of paying it back, his master ordered him to be sold, along with his wife, his children, and all his property, in payment of the debt. At that, the servant fell down, did him homage, and said, 'Be patient with me, and I will pay you back in full.' Moved with compassion the master of that servant let him go and forgave him the loan. When that servant had left, he found one of his fellow servants who owed him a much smaller amount. He seized him and started to choke him, demanding, 'Pay back what you owe.' Falling to his knees, his fellow servant begged him, 'Be patient with me, and I will pay you back.' But he refused. Instead, he had the fellow servant put in prison until he paid back the debt. Now when his fellow servants saw what had happened, they were deeply disturbed, and went to their master and reported the whole affair. His master summoned him and said to him, 'You wicked servant! I forgave you your entire debt because you begged me to. Should you not have had pity on your fellow servant, as I had pity on you?' Then in anger his master handed him over to the torturers until he should pay back the whole debt. So will my heavenly Father do to you, unless each of you forgives your brother from your heart."

# Meditation (*Meditatio*)

*After the reading, take some time to reflect in silence on one or more of the following questions:*

- What word or words in this passage caught your attention?

- What in this passage comforted you?
- What in this passage challenged you?

*If practicing* lectio divina *as a family or in a group, after the reflection time, invite the participants to share their responses.*

# Prayer (*Oratio*)

*Read the Scripture passage one more time. Bring to the Lord the praise, petition, or thanksgiving that the Word inspires in you.*

# Contemplation (*Contemplatio*)

*Read the Scripture again, followed by this reflection:*

 What conversion of mind, heart, and life is the Lord asking of me?

 *Lord, if my brother sins against me, how often must I forgive? What grudges am I holding? Is there anyone I have shut out of my life?*

*A debtor was brought before him who owed him a huge amount.* What do I owe to the Lord? What does the Lord want me to offer him?

*Should you not have had pity on your fellow servant, as I had pity on you?* How can I share the gift of mercy that God has given me? How can I be an ambassador of reconciliation?

# Closing Prayer

*After a period of silent reflection and/or discussion, all recite the Lord's Prayer and the following:*

> Bless the LORD, O my soul;
>     and all my being, bless his holy name.
> Bless the LORD, O my soul,
>     and forget not all his benefits.
>
> He pardons all your iniquities,
>     heals all your ills.

He redeems your life from destruction,
   crowns you with kindness and compassion.

He will not always chide,
   nor does he keep his wrath forever.
Not according to our sins does he deal with us,
   nor does he requite us according to our crimes.

For as the heavens are high above the earth,
   so surpassing is his kindness toward those who fear him.
As far as the east is from the west,
   so far has he put our transgressions from us.

*From Psalm 103*

# Living the Word This Week

*How can I make my life a gift for others in charity?*

Read *God's Gift of Forgiveness: A Pastoral Exhortation on the Sacrament of Penance and* Reconciliation: *www.usccb.org/ prayer-and-worship/sacraments-and-sacramentals/penance/upload/ Penance-Statement-ENG.pdf.*

# September 20, 2020

*Lectio Divina* for the Twenty-Fifth Week in Ordinary Time

*We begin our prayer:*
In the name of the Father, and of the Son, and of the Holy
Spirit. Amen.

O God, who founded all the commands of your sacred Law
upon love of you and of our neighbor,
grant that, by keeping your precepts,
we may merit to attain eternal life.
Through our Lord Jesus Christ, your Son,
who lives and reigns with you in the unity of the Holy Spirit,
one God, for ever and ever.

*Collect, Twenty-Fifth Sunday in Ordinary Time*

# Reading (*Lectio*)

*Read the following Scripture two or three times.*

Matthew 20:1-16a

Jesus told his disciples this parable: "The kingdom of
heaven is like a landowner who went out at dawn
to hire laborers for his vineyard. After agreeing with
them for the usual daily wage, he sent them into his
vineyard. Going out about nine o'clock, the landowner
saw others standing idle in the marketplace, and
he said to them, 'You too go into my vineyard, and
I will give you what is just.' So they went off. And

he went out again around noon, and around three o'clock, and did likewise. Going out about five o'clock, the landowner found others standing around, and said to them, 'Why do you stand here idle all day?' They answered, 'Because no one has hired us.' He said to them, 'You too go into my vineyard.' When it was evening the owner of the vineyard said to his foreman, 'Summon the laborers and give them their pay, beginning with the last and ending with the first.' When those who had started about five o'clock came, each received the usual daily wage. So when the first came, they thought that they would receive more, but each of them also got the usual wage. And on receiving it they grumbled against the landowner, saying, 'These last ones worked only one hour, and you have made them equal to us, who bore the day's burden and the heat.' He said to one of them in reply, 'My friend, I am not cheating you.

Did you not agree with me for the usual daily wage? Take what is yours and go. What if I wish to give this last one the same as you? Or am I not free to do as I wish with my own money? Are you envious because I am generous?' Thus, the last will be first, and the first will be last."

# Meditation (*Meditatio*)

*After the reading, take some time to reflect in silence on one or more of the following questions:*

- What word or words in this passage caught your attention?

- What in this passage comforted you?
- What in this passage challenged you?

*If practicing* lectio divina *as a family or in a group, after the reflection time, invite the participants to share their responses.*

# Prayer (*Oratio*)

*Read the Scripture passage one more time. Bring to the Lord the praise, petition, or thanksgiving that the Word inspires in you.*

# Contemplation (*Contemplatio*)

*Read the Scripture again, followed by this reflection:*

 What conversion of mind, heart, and life is the Lord asking of me?

 *You too go into my vineyard, and I will give you what is just.* How can I show respect for those who work with and for me? How can I be a force for peace and justice?

*Because no one has hired us.* Who in my community is ignored or forgotten? How can I take notice of those too easily disregarded?

*Are you envious because I am generous?* When do I measure myself against others? How can I be more generous with my time and resources?

# Closing Prayer

*After a period of silent reflection and/or discussion, all recite the Lord's Prayer and the following:*

Every day will I bless you,
    and I will praise your name forever and ever.
Great is the LORD and highly to be praised;
    his greatness is unsearchable.

The LORD is gracious and merciful,
    slow to anger and of great kindness.
The LORD is good to all
    and compassionate toward all his works.

The LORD is just in all his ways
   and holy in all his works.
The LORD is near to all who call upon him,
   to all who call upon him in truth.

*From Psalm 145*

## Living the Word This Week

*How can I make my life a gift for others in charity?*

Learn more about the Church's teaching on labor and the rights of workers: *www.usccb.org/issues-and-action/human-life-and-dignity/labor-employment/index.cfm.*

# September 27, 2020

Lectio Divina for the Twenty-Sixth Week in Ordinary Time

*We begin our prayer:*
In the name of the Father, and of the Son, and of the Holy Spirit. Amen.

O God, who manifest your almighty power
above all by pardoning and showing mercy,
bestow, we pray, your grace abundantly upon us
and make those hastening to attain your promises
heirs to the treasures of heaven.
Through our Lord Jesus Christ, your Son,
who lives and reigns with you in the unity of the Holy Spirit,
one God, for ever and ever.

*Collect, Twenty-Sixth Sunday in Ordinary Time*

# Reading (*Lectio*)

*Read the following Scripture two or three times.*

Matthew 21:28-32

Jesus said to the chief priests and elders of the people: "What is your opinion? A man had two sons. He came to the first and said, 'Son, go out and work in the vineyard today.' He said in reply, 'I will not,' but afterwards changed his mind and went. The man came to the other son and gave the same order. He said in reply, 'Yes, sir,' but did not go. Which of

the two did his father's will?" They answered, "The
first." Jesus said to them, "Amen, I say to you, tax
collectors and prostitutes are entering the kingdom
of God before you. When John came to you in the
way of righteousness, you did not believe him; but
tax collectors and prostitutes did. Yet even when you
saw that, you did not later change your minds and
believe him."

# Meditation (*Meditatio*)

*After the reading, take some time to reflect in silence on one or more
of the following questions:*

- What word or words in this passage caught
  your attention?
- What in this passage comforted you?
- What in this passage challenged you?

*If practicing* lectio divina *as a family or in a group, after the
reflection time, invite the participants to share their responses.*

# Prayer (*Oratio*)

*Read the Scripture passage one more time. Bring to the Lord the
praise, petition, or thanksgiving that the Word inspires in you.*

# Contemplation (*Contemplatio*)

*Read the Scripture again, followed by this reflection:*

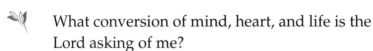 What conversion of mind, heart, and life is the Lord asking of me?

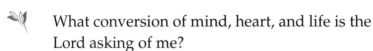 *Son, go out and work in the vineyard today.* What vineyards is God calling me to work in? How can I be more responsive to God's call?

 *He said in reply, "I will not," but afterwards changed his mind and went.* When have I experienced conversion? What parts of my life require change?

*When John came to you in the way of righteousness, you did not believe him.* Who has modeled faith for me? When have I struggled to believe?

# Closing Prayer

*After a period of silent reflection and/or discussion, all recite the Lord's Prayer and the following:*

Your ways, O Lord, make known to me;
    teach me your paths,
guide me in your truth and teach me,
    for you are God my savior.

Remember that your compassion, O Lord,
    and your love are from of old.
The sins of my youth and my frailties remember not;
    in your kindness remember me,
    because of your goodness, O Lord.

Good and upright is the Lord;
    thus he shows sinners the way.
He guides the humble to justice,
    and teaches the humble his way.

*From Psalm 25*

# Living the Word This Week

*How can I make my life a gift for others in charity?*

Invite someone to rediscover their faith: *www.usccb.org/beliefs-and-teachings/how-we-teach/new-evangelization/rediscovering-the-faith/index.cfm.*

# October 4, 2020

*Lectio Divina* for the Twenty-Seventh Week in
Ordinary Time

*We begin our prayer:*
In the name of the Father, and of the Son, and of the Holy
Spirit. Amen.

Almighty ever-living God,
who in the abundance of your kindness
surpass the merits and the desires of those who entreat you,
pour out your mercy upon us
to pardon what conscience dreads
and to give what prayer does not dare to ask.
Through our Lord Jesus Christ, your Son,
who lives and reigns with you in the unity of the Holy Spirit,
one God, for ever and ever.

*Collect, Twenty-Seventh Sunday in Ordinary Time*

# Reading (*Lectio*)

*Read the following Scripture two or three times.*

Matthew 21:33-43

Jesus said to the chief priests and the elders of
the people: "Hear another parable. There was a
landowner who planted a vineyard, put a hedge
around it, dug a wine press in it, and built a tower.
Then he leased it to tenants and went on a journey.

When vintage time drew near, he sent his servants to the tenants to obtain his produce. But the tenants seized the servants and one they beat, another they killed, and a third they stoned. Again he sent other servants, more numerous than the first ones, but they treated them in the same way. Finally, he sent his son to them, thinking, 'They will respect my son.' But when the tenants saw the son, they said to one another, 'This is the heir. Come, let us kill him and acquire his inheritance.' They seized him, threw him out of the vineyard, and killed him. What will the owner of the vineyard do to those tenants when he comes?" They answered him, "He will put those wretched men to a wretched death and lease his vineyard to other tenants who will give him the produce at the proper times." Jesus said to them, "Did you never read in the Scriptures:

*The stone that the builders rejected*
*    has become the cornerstone;*
*by the Lord has this been done,*
*    and it is wonderful in our eyes?*

Therefore, I say to you, the kingdom of God will be taken away from you and given to a people that will produce its fruit."

# Meditation (*Meditatio*)

*After the reading, take some time to reflect in silence on one or more of the following questions:*

- What word or words in this passage caught your attention?

- What in this passage comforted you?
- What in this passage challenged you?

*If practicing* lectio divina *as a family or in a group, after the reflection time, invite the participants to share their responses.*

# Prayer (*Oratio*)

*Read the Scripture passage one more time. Bring to the Lord the praise, petition, or thanksgiving that the Word inspires in you.*

# Contemplation (*Contemplatio*)

*Read the Scripture again, followed by this reflection:*

 What conversion of mind, heart, and life is the Lord asking of me?

 *When vintage time drew near, he sent his servants to the tenants to obtain his produce.* How do I repay God for the good things he has done for me? What is due to God?

*But the tenants seized the servants and one they beat, another they killed, and a third they stoned.* How do I respond to God's message and to those who carry it? How do people respond to me when I share God's word?

 *The stone that the builders rejected has become the cornerstone.* When have I experienced rejection because of my faith? Is the cornerstone of my faith a who or a what?

# Closing Prayer

*After a period of silent reflection and/or discussion, all recite the Lord's Prayer and the following:*

A vine from Egypt you transplanted;
   you drove away the nations and planted it.
It put forth its foliage to the Sea,
   its shoots as far as the River.

Why have you broken down its walls,
   so that every passer-by plucks its fruit,
The boar from the forest lays it waste,
   and the beasts of the field feed upon it?

Once again, O LORD of hosts,
   look down from heaven, and see;
take care of this vine,
   and protect what your right hand has planted
   the son of man whom you yourself made strong.

Then we will no more withdraw from you;
   give us new life, and we will call upon your name.
O LORD, God of hosts, restore us;
   if your face shine upon us, then we shall be saved.

*From Psalm 80*

# Living the Word This Week

*How can I make my life a gift for others in charity?*

Learn more about religious liberty: *www.usccb.org/issues-and-action/religious-liberty/bulletin-inserts.cfm.*

# October 11, 2020

*Lectio Divina* for the Twenty-Eighth Week in
Ordinary Time

*We begin our prayer:*
In the name of the Father, and of the Son, and of the Holy
Spirit. Amen.

May your grace, O Lord, we pray,
at all times go before us and follow after
and make us always determined
to carry out good works.
Through our Lord Jesus Christ, your Son,
who lives and reigns with you in the unity of the Holy Spirit,
one God, for ever and ever.

*Collect, Twenty-Eighth Sunday in Ordinary Time*


# Reading (*Lectio*)

*Read the following Scripture two or three times.*

Matthew 22:1-14

Jesus again in reply spoke to the chief priests and
elders of the people in parables, saying, "The
kingdom of heaven may be likened to a king who
gave a wedding feast for his son. He dispatched his
servants to summon the invited guests to the feast,
but they refused to come. A second time he sent other
servants, saying, 'Tell those invited: "Behold, I have

prepared my banquet, my calves and fattened cattle
are killed, and everything is ready; come to the feast.'"
Some ignored the invitation and went away, one to
his farm, another to his business. The rest laid hold
of his servants, mistreated them, and killed them.
The king was enraged and sent his troops, destroyed
those murderers, and burned their city. Then he said
to his servants, 'The feast is ready, but those who were
invited were not worthy to come. Go out, therefore,
into the main roads and invite to the feast whomever
you find.' The servants went out into the streets and
gathered all they found, bad and good alike, and the
hall was filled with guests. But when the king came in
to meet the guests, he saw a man there not dressed in
a wedding garment. The king said to him, 'My friend,
how is it that you came in here without a wedding
garment?' But he was reduced to silence. Then the king
said to his attendants, 'Bind his hands and feet, and
cast him into the darkness outside, where there will be
wailing and grinding of teeth.' Many are invited, but
few are chosen."


# Meditation (*Meditatio*)

*After the reading, take some time to reflect in silence on one or more*
*of the following questions:*

- What word or words in this passage caught
  your attention?
- What in this passage comforted you?
- What in this passage challenged you?

*If practicing* lectio divina *as a family or in a group, after the*
*reflection time, invite the participants to share their responses.*

# Prayer (*Oratio*)

*Read the Scripture passage one more time. Bring to the Lord the praise, petition, or thanksgiving that the Word inspires in you.*

# Contemplation (*Contemplatio*)

*Read the Scripture again, followed by this reflection:*

 What conversion of mind, heart, and life is the Lord asking of me?

 *He dispatched his servants to summon the invited guests to the feast, but they refused to come.* When was the last time I invited someone to join me at Mass? When have I refused an invitation to grow closer to God?

*The feast is ready, but those who were invited were not worthy to come.* When have I felt unworthy of God's love? When have I made others feel unworthy?

 *Go out, therefore, into the main roads and invite to the feast whomever you find.* Who needs to be invited to greater participation in the Church? How can I be more welcoming to those new to the community?

# Closing Prayer

*After a period of silent reflection and/or discussion, all recite the Lord's Prayer and the following:*

The Lord is my shepherd; I shall not want.
    In verdant pastures he gives me repose;
beside restful waters he leads me;
    he refreshes my soul.

He guides me in right paths
  for his name's sake.
Even though I walk in the dark valley
  I fear no evil; for you are at my side
with your rod and your staff
  that give me courage.

You spread the table before me
  in the sight of my foes;
you anoint my head with oil;
  my cup overflows.

Only goodness and kindness follow me
  all the days of my life;
and I shall dwell in the house of the LORD
  for years to come.

*From Psalm 23*

# Living the Word This Week

*How can I make my life a gift for others in charity?*

Learn more about building intercultural competencies and creating a welcoming environment for all: *www.usccb.org/ issues-and-action/cultural-diversity/intercultural-competencies/ index.cfm.*

# OCTOBER 18, 2020

*Lectio Divina* for the Twenty-Ninth Week in Ordinary Time

*We begin our prayer:*
In the name of the Father, and of the Son, and of the Holy
Spirit. Amen.

Almighty ever-living God,
grant that we may always conform our will to yours
and serve your majesty in sincerity of heart.
Through our Lord Jesus Christ, your Son,
who lives and reigns with you in the unity of the Holy Spirit,
one God, for ever and ever.

*Collect, Twenty-Ninth Sunday in Ordinary Time*

# Reading (*Lectio*)

*Read the following Scripture two or three times.*

Matthew 22:15-21

The Pharisees went off and plotted how they might
entrap Jesus in speech. They sent their disciples to
him, with the Herodians, saying, "Teacher, we know
that you are a truthful man and that you teach the
way of God in accordance with the truth. And you are
not concerned with anyone's opinion, for you do not
regard a person's status. Tell us, then, what is your
opinion: Is it lawful to pay the census tax to Caesar
or not?" Knowing their malice, Jesus said, "Why are

you testing me, you hypocrites? Show me the coin that pays the census tax." Then they handed him the Roman coin. He said to them, "Whose image is this and whose inscription?" They replied, "Caesar's." At that he said to them, "Then repay to Caesar what belongs to Caesar and to God what belongs to God."

# Meditation (*Meditatio*)

*After the reading, take some time to reflect in silence on one or more of the following questions:*

- What word or words in this passage caught your attention?
- What in this passage comforted you?
- What in this passage challenged you?

*If practicing* lectio divina *as a family or in a group, after the reflection time, invite the participants to share their responses.*

# Prayer (*Oratio*)

*Read the Scripture passage one more time. Bring to the Lord the praise, petition, or thanksgiving that the Word inspires in you.*

# Contemplation (*Contemplatio*)

*Read the Scripture again, followed by this reflection:*

What conversion of mind, heart, and life is the Lord asking of me?

*Teacher, we know that you are a truthful man and that you teach the way of God in accordance with the truth.* What opportunities do I have to teach the faith? How can I be more docile to the teaching of the Church?

*And you are not concerned with anyone's opinion, for you do not regard a person's status.* When have I let others' opinion sway me from doing God's will? What biases and prejudices must I eliminate from my thinking?

*Then repay to Caesar what belongs to Caesar and to God what belongs to God.* What role does my faith play in my life as a citizen? How can I be a better steward of all that God has given me?

# Closing Prayer

*After a period of silent reflection and/or discussion, all recite the Lord's Prayer and the following:*

Sing to the Lord a new song;
    sing to the Lord, all you lands.
Tell his glory among the nations;
    among all peoples, his wondrous deeds.

For great is the Lord and highly to be praised;
    awesome is he, beyond all gods.
For all the gods of the nations are things of nought,
    but the Lord made the heavens.

Give to the Lord, you families of nations,
    give to the Lord glory and praise;
give to the Lord the glory due his name!
    Bring gifts, and enter his courts.

Worship the Lord, in holy attire;
    tremble before him, all the earth;
say among the nations: The Lord is king,
    he governs the peoples with equity.

*From Psalm 96*

# Living the Word This Week

*How can I make my life a gift for others in charity?*

Read *Open Wide Our Hearts: An Enduring Call to Love, A Pastoral Letter Against Racism*: *www.usccb.org/issues-and-action/ human-life-and-dignity/racism/upload/open-wide-our-hearts.pdf.*

# OCTOBER 25, 2020

*Lectio Divina* for the Thirtieth Week in Ordinary Time

*We begin our prayer:*
In the name of the Father, and of the Son, and of the Holy
Spirit. Amen.

Almighty ever-living God,
increase our faith, hope and charity,
and make us love what you command,
so that we may merit what you promise.
Through our Lord Jesus Christ, your Son,
who lives and reigns with you in the unity of the Holy Spirit,
one God, for ever and ever.

*Collect, Thirtieth Sunday in Ordinary Time*

# Reading (*Lectio*)

*Read the following Scripture two or three times.*

Matthew 22:34-40

When the Pharisees heard that Jesus had silenced
the Sadducees, they gathered together, and one
of them, a scholar of the law tested him by asking,
"Teacher, which commandment in the law is the
greatest?" He said to him, "You shall love the Lord,
your God, with all your heart, with all your soul, and
with all your mind. This is the greatest and the first
commandment. The second is like it: You shall love

your neighbor as yourself. The whole law and the prophets depend on these two commandments."

## Meditation (*Meditatio*)

*After the reading, take some time to reflect in silence on one or more of the following questions:*

- What word or words in this passage caught your attention?
- What in this passage comforted you?
- What in this passage challenged you?

*If practicing* lectio divina *as a family or in a group, after the reflection time, invite the participants to share their responses.*

## Prayer (*Oratio*)

*Read the Scripture passage one more time. Bring to the Lord the praise, petition, or thanksgiving that the Word inspires in you.*

## Contemplation (*Contemplatio*)

*Read the Scripture again, followed by this reflection:*

 What conversion of mind, heart, and life is the Lord asking of me?

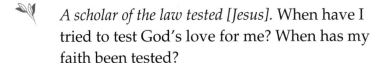 *A scholar of the law tested [Jesus].* When have I tried to test God's love for me? When has my faith been tested?

*You shall love the Lord, your God, with all your heart, with all your soul, and with all your mind.* How can I grow in love for God? How can I express my love for God this week?

*You shall love your neighbor as yourself.* Who is my neighbor? How can I love those God has placed in my path?

# Closing Prayer

*After a period of silent reflection and/or discussion, all recite the Lord's Prayer and the following:*

I love you, O LORD, my strength,
   O LORD, my rock, my fortress, my deliverer.

My God, my rock of refuge,
   my shield, the horn of my salvation, my stronghold!
Praised be the LORD, I exclaim,
   and I am safe from my enemies.

The LORD lives and blessed be my rock!
   Extolled be God my savior.
You who gave great victories to your king
   and showed kindness to your anointed.

*From Psalm 18*

# Living the Word This Week

*How can I make my life a gift for others in charity?*

In anticipation of the general election, pray the Novena for Faithful Citizenship: *www.usccb.org/prayer-and-worship/prayers-and-devotions/prayers/novena-for-faithful-citizenship.cfm.*

# November 1, 2020

*Lectio Divina* for the Solemnity of All Saints

*We begin our prayer:*
In the name of the Father, and of the Son, and of the Holy
Spirit. Amen.

Almighty ever-living God,
by whose gift we venerate in one celebration
the merits of all the Saints,
bestow on us, we pray,
through the prayers of so many intercessors,
an abundance of the reconciliation with you
for which we earnestly long.
Through our Lord Jesus Christ, your Son,
who lives and reigns with you in the unity of the Holy Spirit,
one God, for ever and ever.

*Collect, Solemnity of All Saints*

# Reading (*Lectio*)

*Read the following Scripture two or three times.*

Matthew 5:1-12a

When Jesus saw the crowds, he went up the
mountain, and after he had sat down, his
disciples came to him. He began to teach them, saying:

"Blessed are the poor in spirit,
    for theirs is the Kingdom of heaven.
Blessed are they who mourn,
    for they will be comforted.
Blessed are the meek,
    for they will inherit the land.
Blessed are they who hunger and thirst for righteousness,
    for they will be satisfied.
Blessed are the merciful,
    for they will be shown mercy.
Blessed are the clean of heart,
    for they will see God.
Blessed are the peacemakers,
    for they will be called children of God.
Blessed are they who are persecuted for the sake of
        righteousness,
    for theirs is the Kingdom of heaven.
Blessed are you when they insult you and persecute you
    and utter every kind of evil against you falsely because of
        me.
Rejoice and be glad,
    for your reward will be great in heaven."

# Meditation (*Meditatio*)

*After the reading, take some time to reflect in silence on one or more
of the following questions:*

- What word or words in this passage caught
  your attention?
- What in this passage comforted you?
- What in this passage challenged you?

*If practicing* lectio divina *as a family or in a group, after the reflection time, invite the participants to share their responses.*

# Prayer (*Oratio*)

*Read the Scripture passage one more time. Bring to the Lord the praise, petition, or thanksgiving that the Word inspires in you.*

# Contemplation (*Contemplatio*)

*Read the Scripture again, followed by this reflection:*

 What conversion of mind, heart, and life is the Lord asking of me?

 *Blessed are the poor in spirit, / for theirs is the Kingdom of heaven.* When have I put my trust in the things of this world instead of in God? How can I live with greater simplicity and generosity?

*Blessed are they who hunger and thirst for righteousness, / for they will be satisfied.* For what do I hunger? How does God satisfy those hungers?

 *Blessed are the merciful, / for they will be shown mercy.* From whom do I need to ask forgiveness? Whom do I need to forgive?

# Closing Prayer

*After a period of silent reflection and/or discussion, all recite the Lord's Prayer and the following:*

The LORD's are the earth and its fullness;
    the world and those who dwell in it.
For he founded it upon the seas
    and established it upon the rivers.

Who can ascend the mountain of the LORD?
    or who may stand in his holy place?

One whose hands are sinless, whose heart is clean,
who desires not what is vain.

He shall receive a blessing from the LORD,
a reward from God his savior.
Such is the race that seeks him,
that seeks the face of the God of Jacob.

*From Psalm 24*

# Living the Word This Week

*How can I make my life a gift for others in charity?*

Read Pope Francis's apostolic exhortation on holiness, *Rejoice and Be Glad*: *http://w2.vatican.va/content/francesco/en/apost_exhortations/documents/papa-francesco_esortazione-ap_20180319_gaudete-et-exsultate.html.*

# November 8, 2020

*Lectio Divina* for the Thirty-Second Week in Ordinary Time

*We begin our prayer:*
In the name of the Father, and of the Son, and of the Holy
Spirit. Amen.

Almighty and merciful God,
graciously keep from us all adversity,
so that, unhindered in mind and body alike,
we may pursue in freedom of heart
the things that are yours.
Through our Lord Jesus Christ, your Son,
who lives and reigns with you in the unity of the Holy Spirit,
one God, for ever and ever.

*Collect, Thirty-Second Sunday in Ordinary Time*

# Reading (*Lectio*)

*Read the following Scripture two or three times.*

Matthew 25:1-13

Jesus told his disciples this parable: "The kingdom of
heaven will be like ten virgins who took their lamps
and went out to meet the bridegroom. Five of them
were foolish and five were wise. The foolish ones,
when taking their lamps, brought no oil with them, but
the wise brought flasks of oil with their lamps. Since
the bridegroom was long delayed, they all became

drowsy and fell asleep. At midnight, there was a cry, 'Behold, the bridegroom! Come out to meet him!' Then all those virgins got up and trimmed their lamps. The foolish ones said to the wise, 'Give us some of your oil, for our lamps are going out.' But the wise ones replied, 'No, for there may not be enough for us and you. Go instead to the merchants and buy some for yourselves.' While they went off to buy it, the bridegroom came and those who were ready went into the wedding feast with him. Then the door was locked. Afterwards the other virgins came and said, 'Lord, Lord, open the door for us!' But he said in reply, 'Amen, I say to you, I do not know you.' Therefore, stay awake, for you know neither the day nor the hour."

# Meditation (*Meditatio*)

*After the reading, take some time to reflect in silence on one or more of the following questions:*

- What word or words in this passage caught your attention?
- What in this passage comforted you?
- What in this passage challenged you?

*If practicing* lectio divina *as a family or in a group, after the reflection time, invite the participants to share their responses.*

# Prayer (*Oratio*)

*Read the Scripture passage one more time. Bring to the Lord the praise, petition, or thanksgiving that the Word inspires in you.*

# Contemplation (*Contemplatio*)

*Read the Scripture again, followed by this reflection:*

 What conversion of mind, heart, and life is the Lord asking of me?

 *Five of them were foolish and five were wise.* How have I been foolish this week? How have I been wise?

 *Since the bridegroom was long delayed, they all became drowsy and fell asleep.* How has my practice of my faith become "drowsy" or apathetic?

*Therefore, stay awake, for you know neither the day nor the hour.* Am I ready to greet the Lord at the end of my earthly life? How am I preparing to meet him?

# Closing Prayer

*After a period of silent reflection and/or discussion, all recite the Lord's Prayer and the following:*

O God, you are my God whom I seek;
   for you my flesh pines and my soul thirsts
   like the earth, parched, lifeless and without water.

Thus have I gazed toward you in the sanctuary
   to see your power and your glory,
For your kindness is a greater good than life;
   my lips shall glorify you.

Thus will I bless you while I live;
   lifting up my hands, I will call upon your name.
As with the riches of a banquet shall my soul be satisfied,
   and with exultant lips my mouth shall praise you.

I will remember you upon my couch,
   and through the night-watches I will meditate on you:
You are my help,
   and in the shadow of your wings I shout for joy.

*From Psalm 63*

# Living the Word This Week

*How can I make my life a gift for others in charity?*

Reflect on the end of our earthly life and what the Church teaches about the four last things: death, judgment, heaven, and hell: *http://ccc.usccb.org/flipbooks/uscca/#178.*

# November 15, 2020

*Lectio Divina* for the Thirty-Third Week in Ordinary Time

*We begin our prayer:*
In the name of the Father, and of the Son, and of the Holy
Spirit. Amen.

Grant us, we pray, O Lord our God,
the constant gladness of being devoted to you,
for it is full and lasting happiness
to serve with constancy
the author of all that is good.
Through our Lord Jesus Christ, your Son,
who lives and reigns with you in the unity of the Holy Spirit,
one God, for ever and ever.

*Collect, Thirty-Third Sunday in Ordinary Time*

# Reading (*Lectio*)

*Read the following Scripture two or three times.*

Matthew 25:14-30

Jesus told his disciples this parable: "A man going
on a journey called in his servants and entrusted
his possessions to them. To one he gave five talents; to
another, two; to a third, one--to each according to his
ability. Then he went away. Immediately the one who
received five talents went and traded with them, and
made another five. Likewise, the one who received

two made another two. But the man who received one went off and dug a hole in the ground and buried his master's money.

"After a long time the master of those servants came back and settled accounts with them. The one who had received five talents came forward bringing the additional five. He said, 'Master, you gave me five talents. See, I have made five more.' His master said to him, 'Well done, my good and faithful servant. Since you were faithful in small matters, I will give you great responsibilities. Come, share your master's joy.' Then the one who had received two talents also came forward and said, 'Master, you gave me two talents. See, I have made two more.' His master said to him, 'Well done, my good and faithful servant. Since you were faithful in small matters, I will give you great responsibilities. Come, share your master's joy.' Then the one who had received the one talent came forward and said, 'Master, I knew you were a demanding person, harvesting where you did not plant and gathering where you did not scatter; so out of fear I went off and buried your talent in the ground. Here it is back.' His master said to him in reply, 'You wicked, lazy servant! So you knew that I harvest where I did not plant and gather where I did not scatter? Should you not then have put my money in the bank so that I could have got it back with interest on my return? Now then! Take the talent from him and give it to the one with ten. For to everyone who has, more will be given and he will grow rich; but from the one who has not, even what he has will be taken away. And throw this useless servant into the darkness outside, where there will be wailing and grinding of teeth.'"

# Meditation (*Meditatio*)

*After the reading, take some time to reflect in silence on one or more of the following questions:*

- What word or words in this passage caught your attention?
- What in this passage comforted you?
- What in this passage challenged you?

*If practicing* lectio divina *as a family or in a group, after the reflection time, invite the participants to share their responses.*


# Prayer (*Oratio*)

*Read the Scripture passage one more time. Bring to the Lord the praise, petition, or thanksgiving that the Word inspires in you.*


# Contemplation (*Contemplatio*)

*Read the Scripture again, followed by this reflection:*

 What conversion of mind, heart, and life is the Lord asking of me?

*A man going on a journey called in his servants and entrusted his possessions to them.* What gifts has God entrusted to me? How am I using those gifts?

 *Since you were faithful in small matters, I will give you great responsibilities. Come, share your master's joy.* How can I be more faithful in prayer and participation in the Church's mission? How does my faith bring me joy?

 *So out of fear I went off and buried your talent in the ground.* How do my fears keep me from living the life God calls me to live? How have I ignored my talents and those of others?

# Closing Prayer

*After a period of silent reflection and/or discussion, all recite the Lord's Prayer and the following:*

Blessed are you who fear the LORD,
    who walk in his ways!
For you shall eat the fruit of your handiwork;
    blessed shall you be, and favored.

Your wife shall be like a fruitful vine
    in the recesses of your home;
Your children like olive plants
    around your table.

Behold, thus is the man blessed
    who fears the LORD.
The LORD bless you from Zion:
    may you see the prosperity of Jerusalem
    all the days of your life.

*From Psalm 128*

# Living the Word This Week

*How can I make my life a gift for others in charity?*

Research volunteer opportunities in your parish, diocese, or community and put your talents to work for the common good.

# November 22, 2020

*Lectio Divina* for the Solemnity of Our Lord Jesus Christ, King of the Universe

*We begin our prayer:*
In the name of the Father, and of the Son, and of the Holy Spirit. Amen.

Stir up the will of your faithful, we pray, O Lord,
that, striving more eagerly
to bring your divine work to fruitful completion,
they may receive in greater measure
the healing remedies your kindness bestows.
Through our Lord Jesus Christ, your Son,
who lives and reigns with you in the unity of the Holy Spirit,
one God, for ever and ever.

*Collect, Thirty-Fourth Week in Ordinary Time*

# Reading (*Lectio*)

*Read the following Scripture two or three times.*

Matthew 25:31-46

Jesus said to his disciples: "When the Son of Man comes in his glory, and all the angels with him, he will sit upon his glorious throne, and all the nations will be assembled before him. And he will separate them one from another, as a shepherd separates the sheep from the goats. He will place the sheep on his right and the goats on his left. Then the king will say to those on his right, 'Come, you who are blessed by my Father. Inherit the kingdom prepared for you from the foundation of the world. For I was hungry and you gave me food, I was thirsty and you gave me drink, a stranger and you welcomed me, naked and you clothed me, ill and you cared for me, in prison and you visited me.' Then the righteous will answer him and say, 'Lord, when did we see you hungry and feed you, or thirsty and give you drink? When did we see you a stranger and welcome you, or naked and clothe you? When did we see you ill or in prison, and visit you?' And the king will say to them in reply, 'Amen, I say to you, whatever you did for one of the least brothers of mine, you did for me.' Then he will say to those on his left, 'Depart from me, you accursed, into the eternal fire prepared for the devil and his angels. For I was hungry and you gave me no food, I was thirsty and you gave me no drink, a stranger and you gave me no welcome, naked and you gave me no clothing, ill and in prison, and you did not care for me.' Then they will answer and say, 'Lord, when did we see you hungry or thirsty or a stranger or naked or ill or in prison, and not minister to your needs?' He will answer them, 'Amen, I say to you, what you did not do for one of these least ones, you did not do for me.' And these will go off to eternal punishment, but the righteous to eternal life."

# Meditation (*Meditatio*)

*After the reading, take some time to reflect in silence on one or more of the following questions:*

- What word or words in this passage caught your attention?
- What in this passage comforted you?
- What in this passage challenged you?

*If practicing* lectio divina *as a family or in a group, after the reflection time, invite the participants to share their responses.*

# Prayer (*Oratio*)

*Read the Scripture passage one more time. Bring to the Lord the praise, petition, or thanksgiving that the Word inspires in you.*

# Contemplation (*Contemplatio*)

*Read the Scripture again, followed by this reflection:*

What conversion of mind, heart, and life is the Lord asking of me?

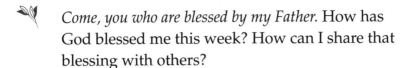 *Come, you who are blessed by my Father.* How has God blessed me this week? How can I share that blessing with others?

*Lord, when did we see you?* When have I seen the Lord acting in my life? How can I make the Lord more visible to those I meet?

*Amen, I say to you, whatever you did for one of the least brothers of mine, you did for me.* What acts of kindness and mercy have I performed this week? What opportunities for kindness and mercy have I let slip away?

# Closing Prayer

*After a period of silent reflection and/or discussion, all recite the Lord's Prayer and the following:*

> The LORD is my shepherd; I shall not want.
> In verdant pastures he gives me repose.
>
> Beside restful waters he leads me;
> he refreshes my soul.
> He guides me in right paths
> for his name's sake.
>
> You spread the table before me
> in the sight of my foes;
> you anoint my head with oil;
> my cup overflows.
>
> Only goodness and kindness follow me
> all the days of my life;
> and I shall dwell in the house of the LORD
> for years to come.

*From Psalm 23*

# Living the Word This Week

*How can I make my life a gift for others in charity?*

Commit to performing the corporal works of mercy in the coming month(s): *www.usccb.org/beliefs-and-teachings/how-we-teach/new-evangelization/jubilee-of-mercy/the-corporal-works-of-mercy.cfm.*